COALITION POLITICS
THE INDIAN EXPERIENCE

About the Author

N. Jose Chander is presently a Visiting Professor of Political Science at the School of International Relations, Mahatma Gandhi University, Kerala. He was, earlier, Professor of Political Science and Director of the Institute of Distance Education, University of Kerala. Also, he was Dean, Faculty of Social Sciences, University of Kerala. He has authored many books including *Legislative Process in Kerala*; *Dynamics of State Politics;* and *Management of Distance Education*. He has participated and presented papers in various national and international conferences.

COALITION POLITICS
The Indian Experience

N. JOSE CHANDER

CONCEPT PUBLISHING COMPANY, NEW DELHI-110059

ISBN-81-8069-092-X

First Published 2004

Published and Printed by
Ashok Kumar Mittal
Concept Publishing Company
A/15-16, Commercial Block, Mohan Garden
NEW DELHI-110059 (India)

Phones : 25351460, 25351794
Fax : 0091-11-25357103
E-mail : publishing@conceptpub.com

PREFACE

The Indian polity was moulded on the British pattern, but the societal forces reshaped it, particularly in the areas of parliamentary performance and of the party system. The emergence of a multi-polar power centre and of innumerable political parties within a unified political system compelled the restructuring of the polity to suit the pressures of coalition politics. The present research focuses on the demands, stresses and constraints of coalitional politics in the changed circumstances and covers political developments to the end of year 2000.

I have been able to undertake this study owing to a Research Fellowship awarded to me by the Lok Sabha Secretariat. I am thankful to the Hon'ble Speaker of the Lok Sabha and Hon'ble Members of the Fellowship Committee for approving the research proposal. Officers and staff of the Lok Sabha Secretariat, particularly of the Parliament Library have been helpful in providing me with facilities without which I would not have been able to complete this study in two years' time. I have been able to make use of the books, journals and the files of newspaper cuttings available with the Parliament Library. Among the officers, I would like to make special mention of Sri G.C. Malhotra, Secretary-General of the Lok Sabha, Dr. A.K. Pande, Retired Additional Secretary, Lok Sabha, Sri John Joseph, Additional Secretary and Member Secretary of the Fellowship Committee, Sri N.K. Sapra, Director, Sri R.T. Pillai, Deputy Director and Sri R.L. Shali, Deputy Director of the Press and Public Relations Department, Sri A.K. Datta, the Librarian, the staff of the Parliament Library, the staff of the I.I.P.A. Library, New Delhi and the staff of the Public Library, Kottayam, Kerala. I must also thank my friend Prof. T.R.S. Iyer for kindly scanning through the script and making suggestions for linguistic improvement. At the same time, I would like to make it clear that I am wholly and personally responsible for the errors or inaccuracies, if any, that might appear in the work.

N. JOSE CHANDER

CONTENTS

LIST OF ABBREVIATIONS

AGP	-	Assam Gana Parishad
AIADMK	-	All India Dravida Munnetra Kazhagom
AICC	-	All India Congress Committee
BJD	-	Biju Janata Dal
BJP	-	Bharatiya Janata Party
BJS	-	Bharatiya Jan Sangh
BKD	-	Bharatiya Kranti Dal
BLD	-	Bharatiya Lok Dal
BSP	-	Bahujan Samaj Party
CFD	-	Congress for Democracy
Congress (I)	-	Congress (Indira)
Congress (O)	-	Congress (Organisation)
Congress (R)	-	Congress (Ruling)
CPI	-	Communist Party of India
CPI (M)	-	Communist Party of India (Marxist)
CPI (M-L)	-	Communist Party of India (Marxist - Leninist)
DMK	-	Dravida Munnetra Kazhagom
FB	-	Forward Bloc
HVP	-	Haryana Vikas Party
INDF	-	Indian National Democratic Front
INLD	-	Indian National Lok Dal
ISP	-	Indian Socialist Party
IUML	-	Indian Union Muslim League
Janata Dal (S)	-	Janata Dal (Secular)
Janata Dal (U)	-	Janata Dal (United)
JP	-	Janata Party
KC (J)	-	Kerala Congress (Joseph)
KC (M)	-	Kerala Congress (Mani)
KPCC	-	Kerala Pradesh Congress Committee
KTP	-	Karshaka Thozhilali Party
LF	-	Left Front
LDF	-	Left Democratic Front
MDMK	-	Marumalarchi Dravida Munnetra Kazhagom
MPVC	-	Madhya Pradesh Vikas Congress

NC	-	National Conference
NCP	-	Nationalist Congress Party
NDA	-	National Democratic Alliance
NDP	-	National Democratic Party
NF	-	National Front
PEPSU	-	Patiala and East Punjab States Union
PMK	-	Pattali Makkal Katchi
PSP	-	Praja Socialist Party
PULF	-	People's United Left Front
RCPI	-	Revolutionary Communist Party of India
RJD	-	Rashtriya Janata Dal
RSP	-	Revolutionary Socialist Party
RSS	-	Rashtriya Swayam Sevak Sangh
SAD	-	Shiromani Akali Dal
SP	-	Samajwadi Party
SRP	-	Socialist Republican Party
SS	-	Shiva Sena
SSP	-	Samyukta Socialist Party
SVD	-	Samyukta Vidhayak Dal
SUCI	-	Socialist Unity Centre of India
TDP	-	Telugu Desam Party
TMC	-	Tamil Manila Congress
TRC	-	Tamizhaka Rajeev Gandhi Congress
UF	-	United Front
UDF	-	United Democratic Front
ULF	-	United Left Front
VHP	-	Viswa Hindu Parishad

1

COALITION POLITICS IN THE PARLIAMENTARY CONTEXT

A Theoretical Framework

The classical paradigm of parliamentary democracy consists of an elected representative Parliament which is supreme, a Cabinet collectively responsible to Parliament, a Prime Minister who is supreme within the Cabinet and an organised opposition within the Parliament. It was assumed that the majority would form the government and the minority would function as the opposition. Problems arose when no party could secure enough majority to form a single-party government, and in such circumstances the alternative was the coalition or multi-party government. This situation invariably leads to some changes in the traditional paradigm of parliamentary democracy. The composition of Cabinet, the nature of its working, the style of the Prime Minister/Chief Minister, the character of electoral politics and the party system, and even the composition of the legislature to a limited extent are likely to be affected by the nature of coalition politics. Although the UK had brief spells of coalition governments, they did not last long enough to change the institutional character. It is left to other countries that are compelled to work continuous coalitions to modify the parliamentary institutions.

Anglo-Saxon countries generally look at coalition government as an aberration, while on the continent of Europe it is the norm. By the middle of 1983 only three European democracies — Britain, Spain and Greece — had single-party majority governments; the rest were ruled either by minority governments or by coalitions.[1] According to Bogdanor, it is hardly possible to understand European political systems without taking into account the working of coalitions. Accepted generalisations about Cabinet government, the role of legislatures and political parties all demand a fresh appraisal in the light of the exigencies of coalition politics. The processes of government formation and dissolution, the role of the Head of State and the working of the Cabinet are all likely to be affected by the coalitions, and the conventions regulating these processes may well differ from those operative in countries enjoying single-party government. In addition, strategies of political parties are likely to be affected by the knowledge that they will be unlikely to win power on their own but will have to share power with like-minded allies. The dynamics of a multi-party system in which coalition is the norm will, therefore, inevitably prove more complex than those in a system of the Westminster type with its presumption of two parties alternating in office, each in turn enjoying the full plenitude of power and patronage.

Coalition building between two or more parties has been frequent in Europe. Between 1990 and 1995 there were no less than 91 Cabinets in office, of which 19 were single-party governments, 68 multi-party governments and 4 caretaker governments.[2] Nevertheless they have not institutionalised coalition politics apart from the parliamentary system. Switzerland is the only exception in Europe with a permanent coalition government by means of its seven-member Federal Council, elected for a fixed four-year term by the Federal Assembly on a party proportional basis. Once the election results are known in Switzerland, it is a question of simple arithmetic as to how the Cabinet seats will be distributed among the parties. The process of Cabinet formation here does not create clear winners and losers.[3] As a result stability is very high in the Swiss case, especially since there exists no vote of non-confidence.

Parliamentarism reigns in Europe but varies from country to country as regards some basic structures and practices. According to Jan-Erik Lane and Svante O. Ersson, the institutions of parliamentarism may vary in relation to the legal requirements for: (i) Cabinet investiture or the procedure for appointing a Premier or government; (ii) a vote of no-confidence by Parliament in relation to the government; (iii) the request for a vote of confidence by the Premier; and (iv) the dissolution of Parliament in order that new elections be held.[4] In the UK there are few restrictions on how these four mechanisms of parliamentarism may be employed, whereas in other countries they are more regulated. The German requirement for a 'constructive vote of non-confidence' is one example which is practised also in Spain where Parliament is restricted to bringing down a government only if it can support a new one. Another instance is the French institution of the block vote, where the Premier may demand that a bill be voted on its entirety, and its rejection by Parliament entails that the Cabinet will step down. Finally, the prerogative of the Premier to dissolve Parliament may be restricted by rules that either stipulate specific circumstances, such as a successful motion of non-confidence, or place the final decision with someone else such as the President in countries with strong presidentialism.

Lane and Ersson distinguish between three types of coalition governments depending on how large the parliamentary support is.[5] They are: (i) minority or less than 50 per cent support; (ii) small majority or more than 50 per cent and less than 60 per cent support; (iii) grand coalitions or oversized governments with more than 60 per cent support. The cut off point of 60 per cent in this classification is arbitrary. In the Indian situation this may be raised to 67 per cent or two-third majority, as two-third majority is required for passing constitutional amendments. The minority model tends to prevail in the Scandinavian countries, whereas grand coalitions are to be found in the so-called consociational countries in Central Europe on the one hand and in the new democracies in Eastern Europe on the other.[6] Minority governments have existed in India both at the Centre and in some States, but majority governments have been the rule rather than the exception.

The level of political stability achieved in the post-1949 European democracies can be measured by the average life-span of governments. According to an estimate, most of the elected Cabinets have survived for periods of considerable length.[7] The mean survival score in Germany has been 37 months and has been significantly higher than in Italy (13 months), Belgium (22 months) and the Netherlands (27 months). In most cases in Germany, the elected government remained in office throughout the period, but there have been exceptions to the rule, as in 1972 and in 1982 when a vote of confidence made way for the dissolution of Parliament before the full term.

Lawrence C. Dodd examines in his *Coalitions in Parliamentary Government* the arguments of eminent scholars from Lowell to Blondel who have asserted that coalition governments are bound to be short-lived.[8] A. Lawrence Lowell had argued in his *Governments and Parties in Continental Europe* (1896) that "the parliamentary system will give a country strong and efficient government only in case the majority consists of a single-party". This thesis has been reaffirmed subsequently by several political scientists in their works. Lord Bryce says in *Modern Democracies* (1921) that a government formed by a coalition of parties is bound to be weak because of the unstable and conflicting character of the compromise involved. Harold J. Laski upholds, in *Parliamentary Government in England* (1938), that durable government requires a majority party system and argues that the multi-party system either results in a coalition with its "inherent erosion of principles" or provides a minority government which is likely to be weak. Maurice Duverger, in his *Political Parties* (1951) asserts that multi-partyism weakens the government in a parliamentary regime. The absence of a majority party necessitates the creation of heterogeneous Cabinets with "limited objectives" and "lukewarm measures". Jean Blondel says that the duration of Cabinet governments is always influenced by the type of party system prevailing in the country and that one-party government is the factor contributing most decisively to the stability of governments.[9] He also says that coalition, small or large, appears directly antagonistic to stability. Scholars from Bryce to Duverger upheld Lowell's thesis by comparing the parliamentary experiences of France and Weimar Germany to those of the UK, implicitly accepting that the former were typical multi-party regimes while the latter was typical of a majority party system. Jean Blondel and Hans Daalder made an advancement by bringing more countries under examination. Blondel analysed the behaviour in seventeen Western parliamentary democracies from 1946 to 1966, focusing on the average differences in Cabinet durability between party systems; Daalder analysed ten smaller European democracies from 1918 to 1969. Several other writers too have contributed to the analysis of multi-partyism resulting in what Dodd calls "the myth of multi-partyism" which implies: (i) governments in multi-party Parliaments must be minority Cabinets, coalition Cabinets, or both; (ii) minority and coalition Cabinets are, by their very nature, bound to be transient; and (iii) multi-party systems are undesirable as they produce only transient governments.[10] Dodd himself analysed the politics of seventeen European countries from 1919 to 1974 and observed: "While the durability of cabinets may be low for all multi-party parliaments, a large number of durable cabinets have survived in multi-party regimes."[11] He further says that while some multi-party Parliaments produce durable Cabinets, other multi-party Parliaments produce transient Cabinets. This implies that durability depends not merely on the number of parties, but on a variety of factors. These factors are what constitute the political culture of a country. So whether a coalition government will be durable in a multi-party system or not depends on the political culture of the country concerned.

A coalition is an alliance of parties formed for the purpose of contesting elections jointly and/or forming a government and managing the governance by a process of sharing power. So coalition implies co-operation between political parties and this co-operation may take place at one or more of three different levels —electoral, parliamentary and governmental. Parliamentary coalitions occur, according to Bogdanor, when no single-party gains a majority and the party asked to form the government prefers to rule as a minority government on an understanding with another for external support.[12] Such an arrangement may be for a long period or for a limited period with a definite date of termination as with the Lib-Lab pact in Great Britain in 1977-78. It is also possible when a government seeks support from different parties for different items of legislation—a method much used in Denmark where it is known as government by 'jumping majorities'. Finally, a minority government might survive without support on a basis of toleration by the opposition parties which do not vote it out for tactical reasons. This was in general the situation of the three Labour minority governments in Britain in 1924, 1929-31 and 1974. In Belgium, the Netherlands and Germany majority coalition rather than minority government is the invariable rule. In Denmark and to a lesser extent in the other Scandinavian countries, minorities may result from the process of government formation. In Italy also single-party governments have been formed and sustained by support from outside. Nevertheless in both Scandinavia and Italy majority coalition is almost always the preferred type. Japan too has experimented with coalition governments since 1993 and in spite of frequent changes of government majority coalition has been the order.[13] In India the governments led by Charan Singh, Chandrasekhar and Deve Gowda had been sustained by Congress support from outside and that of V.P. Singh supported by BJP. In these cases the support had been issue-based as they claimed.

Electoral coalition is formed by two or more parties to fight the elections jointly against a common enemy. This may range from electoral alliance between parties at the national level to a mere understanding at the constituency level. Such coalitions need not necessarily last beyond the elections after which the parties may consider themselves free to make new alliances to form the government. The existence and nature of such coalitions will depend upon the character of the electoral system.[14] Certain electoral systems favour a coalition formation phase before elections rather than after them, a matter that has a fundamental impact on the politics of coalition.[15]

The governmental coalition is a "power sharing" coalition and it occurs when two or more parties, none of which is able to win a majority of its own, combine to form a majority government. The parties comprising such coalitions need not necessarily join together in an electoral pact; they may continue to compete electorally with their own coalition partners. This sort of power sharing coalitions are generally familiar to continental Europe, but comparatively unknown to British politics.[16] In fact, power sharing is the end of all coalitions and, therefore, it is the ultimate stage to be achieved in the election process. Any arrangement that stops short of the ultimate stage lacks commitment. Finally, there are what may be called 'integral' coalitions that link parties through the election process, parliamentary performance and governance. Continuous collaboration and cohesion of allies through the above stages of the political process make them constitute stable coalitions while preserving separate identity of the parties.

Vernon Bogdanor likes to look at coalition government as "a particular form of executive rule separate from both presidential government and from the classical model of Cabinet government as adumbrated by authorities such as Bagehot and Morley."[17] He asserts that a coalition government is more than a modified form of parliamentary government, having its own conventions and rules, all emerging from the fundamental principle of power sharing. According to him the impact of coalition government will be apparent throughout the whole of the political system, so that "the working of institutions such as the Cabinet and the legislature will prove very different from that of their counterparts in systems dominated by the Westminster model." He points out some areas of government wherein coalition politics has made significant deviation from the Westminster model. These relate to the following:

(i) *The role of the Head of State* : In a coalitional system the Head of State is always liable to find himself playing a more active role in government formation than is customary in Britain or in other countries where single-party majority government is the rule.

(ii) *Political homogeneity* : In a coalitional government ministers are invariably drawn from different political parties and hence they represent different and even contradictory viewpoints.

(iii) *Collective responsibility* : It is possible to maintain collective responsibility within a coalition Cabinet with the Prime Minister as the keystone. But it is harder to achieve this ideal in a coalition government than in a single party government.

(iv) *The role of the Prime Minister* : The Prime Minister of a coalition government is neither able to select his colleagues nor exercise control over them.

(v) *The need for party discipline* : A coalition government is likely to be less able to afford breaches of party discipline than a single-party government. The coalition partners are bound by an agreement, tacit or open, on policy and performance, and dissenting votes by any backbencher may threaten the government's majority as well as the very basis of the coalition.

Many countries today have accepted coalition politics, but their constitutions are conspicuously silent on coalition governments which are derived from the exigencies of multi-party politics. Some constitutions, however, contain provisions which facilitate the formation of coalition governments. Germany is the most notable example which indirectly promotes coalition building by the constitutional provisions for a powerful Chancellor, constructive vote of no-confidence, regulation of parties, possibility of outlawing a disloyal opposition, etc. Coalition building in the Federal Republic of Germany was influenced by factors such as the political culture, the geopolitical situation of the country, the functioning of federalism and the development of large catch-all parties.[18] The Belgian Constitution provides for the equal representation in government, with the exception of the Prime Minister, of the French speaking and Dutch speaking members of Parliament.[19] The Constitution further says that on issues related to the language, legislation must be passed with a majority vote within each linguistic group of both Houses, provided the majority of members of each group are present and the total votes in favour of the two linguistic groups attain two-thirds of the votes cast. Apart from constitutional provisions, there are a number of other statutory and institutional factors in European States that might influence the formation of coalition politics, like the electoral system and rules relating to the formation and defeat of governments. A number of West European constitutions, for example, require that an incoming government should survive an investiture vote. This may be sometimes an informal convention, still it makes a major difference to the politics of coalition in a given system.

Coalitions may be classified as (i) policy pursuit models, and (ii) office seeking models based on objectives, and as (iii) minimum winning models, and (iv) large size models based on strategy.[20] Policy pursuit models are those formed by like-minded parties, *i.e.* parties that have a common policy orientation or ideological background. It is often presumed that coalitions are easily formed to make a government when parties are not at a policy distance from each other. Examples are right wing coalitions and left wing coalitions. A coalition which combines leftist parties and rightist parties is a difficult proposition. But sometimes parties and individual legislators may be interested in the pursuit of power or office in total disregard of ideological considerations. They may argue that as power is an instrument for pursuing policies, power or office is what matters most in politics. Minor parties or uncommitted legislators may play truant and jump from the left front to the right front and *vice versa*, but they tend finally to settle down to a front that is more congenial to them.

William Riker's coalition model is office seeking and purely pragmatic. It involves two profound ideas. First, coalitions tend to be as small as is strictly necessary for winning a simple majority to form a government. A minimum winning coalition stands on the brink so much so that the defection of a single member will make the coalition no longer extant. One advantage of a minimum winning coalition is that the total gains won by the coalition can be distributed in larger shares for each partner participating in the coalition. Hence it is a matter of maximum pay off for the minimum number possible. Second, minimum winning coalitions are less vulnerable to opinion shifts than grand coalitions or minority governments and therefore more durable than the latter. Probably being on the brink, a minimum winning coalition realises the necessity of discipline and cohesion among its ranks. However the office seeking, minimum winning model is more theoretical than practical and it precludes the consideration of political reality or circumstances. In societies with sharp ethnic or other divisions and with innumerable groups and parties representing them, grand or large sized coalitions seem to be in order. In the Indian situation, both at the Centre and in the States, the tendency is to make coalitions large and broad based and therefore the leading parties try to entice into their fold even feeble parties that are not sure of their post-election survival. Probably this is facilitated by three factors. One, the leading parties want to ensure such a large majority as to be representative of vast sections of people in the country. Two, the lack of discipline and cohesion among party legislators fail to assure the continuance of a minimum winning coalition. Three, the factional character of all parties, including the major parties, does not rule out the possibility of defection of members in spite of anti-defection laws that may exist in the country.

Most theoretical models of coalitional behaviour applied in Western Europe have tended to assume a bargaining environment more or less free from constraints. They tend to assume that every arithmetically possible combination has a chance of becoming real, other things being equal. Little or no attention is paid to the specific local circumstances or to the institutional, legal and personal constraints involved. Some constraints are products of very specific local circumstances like personality clashes, ethnic group identities or similar conflicts that deter groups or parties from coming together. In most political systems of Western Europe certain political parties have been treated as political untouchables, being excluded from the bargaining process by all other parties.[21] All such phenomena are available in the Indian society too, having a large and diverse population as in the whole of Europe taken together. Hence these constraints influence the character of coalitional politics in the national political system as well as in each State political system in the country.

In the light of the various studies conducted about the coalition governments of Europe, the Indian experience in coalition politics deserves to be examined. The Indian political system has similarities and differences with the European political systems in general, but the political culture and people being different the political outputs may also be different. Being the largest Parliamentary democracy in the world, India's experiments are of vital importance to the political world.

A good number of scholarly works have been written on political parties and coalition governments during the 20th century based on the experiences of Britain and the European countries. But the classical works have been mostly biased in favour of single-party majoritarian governments and they have regarded multi-party governments as non-durable. More objective and comparative transnational studies appeared towards the end of the century and they seemed to take the coalition phenomenon as natural and related to political culture. The growth of the scientific interest in the study of European coalition politics led to the development of two approaches: the European politics tradition and the game-theoretic tradition. The chief contributor to the latter tradition has been William Riker whose *Theory of Coalitions* (1962) has become the source of the theory of minimum winning coalition.

Lawrence C. Dodd challenges the time-old theory that a durable Cabinet (*Coalitions in Parliamentary Government,* 1976) requires a majority party government and argues for a fundamental alteration in the existing conceptions. Vernon Bogdanor (*Coalition Government in Western Europe* (ed.), 1983) describes the working of coalition governments in the democracies of Western Europe. The influence of coalition politics on Cabinet, Parliament, policy outputs, etc. are studied here in the context of countries like West Germany, Norway Sweden, Denmark, the Netherlands, Belgium, Italy and Ireland. Ian Budge and Hans Keman (*Parties and Democracy – Coalition Formation and Government Functioning in Twenty States,* 1990) analyse the actual behaviour of some four hundred governments in twenty post-war democracies and try to find answers to questions relating to the formation of governments, distribution of portfolios and how parties influence policy. Michael Laver and Norman Schoefield (*Multi-party Government – the Politics of Coalition in Europe,* 1990) have tried to reconcile the theoretical and empirical approaches to the study. Their work offers an accessible approach that bridges the distance between the 'European politics' and 'game theory' traditions of political science. Five basic themes are examined: the identity and motivation of actors in the game; the eventual membership of the coalitions they form; their durability; the pay offs that are shared; and the impact of constitutional, behavioural and historical constraints on the process of coalition bargaining. Jug Steiner's comparative analysis (*European Democracies,* 3rd edition, 1955) is another major contribution in this area. Joseph M. Colomer's edited volume (*Political Institutions in Europe,* 1996) contain several sections on the individual nations of Europe. Jan-Erik Lane and Svante O. Ersson (*European*

Politics : An Introduction, 1996) explains the character and trends of European politics and devotes a major part of the work for the analysis of European coalitions. Bradley Richardson's work (*Japanese Democracy,* 1977) pays attention to the recent coalitional developments in Japanese politics and thus takes a look towards Asia.

About politics in India, innumerable books and articles have been published. But specialist works on coalitional aspects, theory or practice, have been limited in number. A few works deserve mention. K.P. Karunakaran's edited volume (*Coalition Governments in India: Problems and Prospects,* 1975) analyses some theories and concepts about coalition making and gives brief reports about some States in India. S.C. Kashyap's edited work (*Coalition Government and Politics in India,* 1997) broadly examines the question in the context of the United Front coalition at the Centre. D. Sunder Ram's work [*Indian Parliamentary Opposition* (ed), 1996] contains two reprinted articles on coalition politics in India, by Iqbal Narayan and Ramakrishna Hegde written much before coalitions appeared at the Centre. *Indian Politics at the Crossroads* (1998) edited by Anil Kumar Jana presents three chapters dealing with the different aspects of coalition politics. Many articles have been published in various journals dealing with current politics of the country.

There are a few works on coalition politics in the Indian States including Kerala and West Bengal. John P. John (*Coalition Politics in Kerala,* 1983) examines the working of the coalition ministries of the 1950s and 1960s. K.V. Varghese (*UF Government in Kerala 1967-69,* 1978) makes an exhaustive study of the coalition led by E.M. Sankaran Namboodiripad in 1967-69. E.J. Thomas (*Coalition Game Politics in Kerala after Independence,* 1994) looks at coalition politics from the game theory point of view. A. Balakrishnan Nair (*Government and Politics of Kerala,* 1994) makes a comprehensive study of Kerala politics including coalition phases. There are other writers, too, like T.J. Nossiter (*Communism in Kerala: A Study in Political Adaptation,* 1982), N. Jose Chander [*Dynamics of State Politics ––Kerala* (ed), 1986] who have paid attention to some aspects of coalition politics in Kerala. It may be noted here that some

Ph.D. dissertations have been submitted to the University of Kerala which relate to some major aspects of coalition politics. Among them A.A. Sebastian's work (*Role of Chief Minister in Coalition Governments: A Study of Kerala,* 1994) and Raju Abraham's thesis (*Role of Political Parties in State Legislature,* 1990) are outstanding contributions.

Anjali Ghosh (*Peaceful Transition to Power,* 1981) makes a detailed and perceptive study of the coalitional games played by the Communists and non-Communists during 1967-77 in West Bengal. P.R. Choudhary's work (*Left Experiments in West Bengal,* 1985) deals with the political history of West Bengal during two decades — 1960s and 1970s. Surabhi Banerjee's biography of Jyoti Basu (*Jyoti Basu : The Authorised Biography,* 1997) covers the political developments of West Bengal from a biographical perspective. A number of articles have been published on Kerala and West Bengal in current journals and dailies, in addition.

However, no comprehensive and scientific analysis of coalition politics in India as a whole has been attempted so far and the present work aims at filling this gap. The study is divided into six chapters. The first chapter looks at coalition politics from a theoretical perspective and establishes the relevance of the study. Chapter 2 takes an overview of coalitional experiments in various Indian States. Chapter 3 analyses the experiences of the Central Government. Chapter 4 examines the experiences of Kerala State from 1967 and Chapter 5 those of West Bengal State since 1977. Chapter 6 makes general observations based on the study.

NOTES

1. Vernon Bogdanor (ed), *Coalition Government in Western Europe,* (London, 1983), p.1.
2. Lane and Ersson, *European Politics : An Introduction*, Sage (New Delhi, 1996), p. 137.
3. Jug Steiner, *European Democracies,* 3rd edition, Longman (New York, 1995), p. 73.
4. Lane and Ersson, n. (2), p. 104.
5. *Ibid.,* p. 138.
6. *Ibid.,* p. 149.

7. Manfred G. Schmidt, "Germany — the Grand Coalition State" in Joseph M. Colomer (ed), *Political Institutions in Europe,* Routledge (New York, 1996), p. 74.
8. Lawrence C. Dodd, *Coalitions in Parliamentary Government,* Princeton University Press (New Jersey, 1976), p. 7.
9. *Ibid.*, p. 9.
10. *Ibid.*, p. 10.
11. *Ibid.*, p. 13.
12. V. Bogdanor, n. (1), p. 5.
13. Bradley Richardson, *Japanese Democracy,* Yale University Press (New Haven, 1997), p. 88.
14. V. Bogdanor, n. (1), p. 7.
15. Michael Laver and Norman Schofield, *Multi-party Government — The Politics of Coalition in Europe,* OUP (New York, 1990), p. 202.
16. V. Bogdanor, n. (1), p. 11.
17. *Ibid.*, p. 263.
18. Klaus Von Beyme, "Coalition Government in West Germany", in V. Bogdanor, n. (1), p. 34.
19. Michael Laver and Norman Schofield, n. (15), p. 202.
20. Lane and Ersson, n. (2), pp. 135-36.
21. Laver and Schofield, n. (15), p. 200.

2

THE INDIAN PANORAMA

The Indian Union is a federal structure with 28 States, including the three States — Uttaranchal, Jharkhand and Chattisgarh — created in August 2000. There is a Central Government for the whole of the country and State Governments for each of the 28 States. The system of government is parliamentary, the Constitution having made provisions for both Central and State Governments, more or less on a similar pattern. Built on the majoritarian principle of the Westminster model and buttressed by the single-party dominance of the Indian National Congress, the Central and State Governments in India have been able to present a picture of stable parliamentary politics in the first two decades since Independence. However, there have been instances of States lacking in political stability from early 1950s owing to the failure of the major national party — the Indian National Congress — and of the regional parties to muster enough support to form a stable government.

The erstwhile States of Travancore–Cochin and PEPSU were the first two States in the country to form coalition governments after the first State Legislative Assembly elections in December 1951-January 1952. During 1953-67, three more coalition governments appeared: Andhra Pradesh (1953-56), Orissa (1957-62) and Kerala (1960-64). In 1967, eight States formed non-Congress coalition governments, and they were: Kerala, West Bengal, Punjab, Haryana, Uttar Pradesh, Madhya Pradesh, Bihar and Orissa. Of these States, Kerala, West Bengal, Punjab, Bihar and Orissa had fragmented Assemblies after the fourth general election of 1967. In Haryana, UP and MP, the Congress party formed its own governments but they fell owing to defection of members and gave way to coalitions. This trend continued although some of the above States went back to single-party Congress governments. In 1997 the number of

States with coalition governments rose to fourteen, the States being: Kerala, West Bengal, Punjab, Haryana, Uttar Pradesh, Bihar, Maharashtra, Gujarat, Goa, Assam, Tripura, Mizoram, Manipur and Sikkim. In successive elections to the Parliament, the Congress party retained power at the Centre until 1977 when it was replaced by the Janata party which was a hotch-potch union of several parties. The Centre also entered the coalition phase in 1996, having formed the first United Front government which was undoubtedly coalitional in character. Among the above States, Kerala has had the longest experience of stable coalition politics with West Bengal standing second. As their experiences have been unique in Indian politics their coalitional history has been examined in detail in separate chapters. Coalition politics of the other States have had a chequered history, going back and forth between single-party and coalitional forms of government. The experience of the major States are outlined briefly in the following paragraphs of this chapter.

Punjab witnessed the emergence of coalition politics in 1967 when the then ruling Congress party lost majority and the opposition parties formed a coalition government under the leadership of Gurnam Singh.[1] The constituents of the United Front were: Akali Dal (Master Tara Singh Group) 2; Akali Dal (Sant Group) 24; CPI(M) 3; CPI 5; Jan Sangh 9; Republican Party 3; SSP 1 and Independents 6. The CPI(M) gave unconditional support to the Ministry without joining it. Starting with five Ministers, the Cabinet was expanded five times to give representation to the constituents as well as to accommodate defectors from the Congress. However, internal dissensions within the leading Akali group and the manoeuvrings of the Congress from outside led to the rise and fall of four coalition Ministries during the period from 8 March, 1967 to 13 June 1971 with a six months' President's rule and a mid-term poll in February 1969. The second phase of coalition government started after the June 1977 Assembly elections when the electoral alliance of Akali, Janata and CPI(M) parties captured 91 out of 117 seats. The Akalis and the Janata formed the government and the CPI(M) gave external support. This Ministry led by Prakash Singh Badal came to an early end owing to infighting among the Akalis and withdrawal of support by the Janata members on 3 September, 1979 for reasons relating to the then Central Government. The Ministry continued until 17 February 1980 when it was dismissed and President's rule imposed together with eight other States in the wake of the Congress party coming to power at the Centre in January 1980. In the elections that followed to the Punjab Legislative Assembly the Congress secured 63 seats out of 117 and formed a government under Darbara Singh.[2] President's rule was imposed again in 1983, and the next polls were held in September 1985. In this poll the Akalis secured 73 out of 117 seats and formed the government. But this government led by Surjeet Singh Barnala had to face a serious crisis as 27 Akali members left the party and the government had to depend on the support of the Congress(I), BJP, CPI and CPI(M). However, in view of the fast deteriorating law and order situation in the State, the President's rule was declared again on 11 May, 1987.

After another spell of Congress(I) rule, marked by continued infighting of Akali factions and mass scale destruction of human lives, Punjab entered the next phase of a peaceful coalitional politics after the Assembly elections of February 1997. The Shiromani Akali Dal (SAD)-BJP electoral alliance won a near three-fourth majority and formed a coalition government under Prakash Singh Badal as Chief Minister. Although SAD alone has a strength of 74 out of 117, it has preferred to maintain the alliance in running the government for various political reasons. First, it was a pre-electoral alliance and was therefore committed to implementing a common minimum programme. Second, the BJP and the SAD are allies in the National Democratic Alliance at the Centre and have a joint responsibility to work together at the Centre for implementing the national agenda. Third, they have a common interest in sharing power at the Centre and in the State despite the apparently contradictory positions they occupy at the two capitals. The BJP's command over the SAD at the Centre and the superiority of the latter over the former in the State of Punjab make for a see-saw arrangement beneficial to both the parties. To sum up, the coalitional experiments in Punjab during the three decades since 1967 had been chequered by factional infighting in the major parties and the extremist violence let loose by terrorists and the police, resulting in the prolonged breakdown of law and order and the failure of constitutional government. Only when peace was finally restored in late nineties, could coalition politics of the Akalis and the BJP be established as a normal system of parliamentary government. However, the prospects of an alternative government — whether of a single-party or of coalition — do not appear bright in the present circumstances.

Bihar provided another instance of unstable coalition governments during 1967-72. During the five-year period the State had as many as nine governments with the life-span of four days to ten months.[3] Out of these governments, four were anti-Congress coalitions, three Congress-led coalitions and two Congress-supported minority coalitions. A mid-term poll was held in February 1969 which did not make any improvement on the situation. However, with the general elections in March 1972 the Congress (I) came back to power on its own, putting an end to the era of coalition governments. The second phase of coalition politics in Bihar started after the Legislative Assembly elections held in February 2000. The Rashtriya Janata Dal (RJD) — a breakaway wing of the former Janata Dal – led by Laloo Prasad Yadav and his wife Rabri Devi who was Chief Minister lost majority but gained the largest number of seats. Ignoring the claim of RJD to be invited to form the government, the Governor V.C. Pande played politics to favour the NDA and invited Nitish Kumar who had been elected the leader of the NDA parliamentary party to form the government and prove his majority. However, Nitish Kumar had to make his exit within seven days as he could not win a majority in the Legislative Assembly. Although the Congress (I) and the Left parties had opposed the "corrupt" RJD government in the elections, they offered to support a "secular" RJD government to spite the "communal" NDA. Laloo Prasad Yadav cleverly supported the Congress (I) candidate for Speakership and checked the expected split in the Congress (I) by manipulating the absence of Congress (I) MLAs by keeping them in a Patna hotel.[4] The parties represented in the Assembly today are so fragmented as to foreclose any possibility of single-party government re-emerging.

The State of Orissa was one of the earliest to experiment with coalition government, having formed a coalition of the two largest parties in the Assembly — the Congress and the Ganatantra Parishad — in 1959.[5] After the second general elections in 1957 the Congress party had formed a government of its own under H.K. Mahtab as Chief Minister with the support of the Communists and the Jharkhand party. As problems arose between the Congress and the Communists, the former entered into coalition with the Parishad and formed the first coalition government on 12 May, 1959. The government continued to function for 21 months and finally broke down on 25 February, 1961 owing to factionalism within the Congress. The second coalition government came to power after the fourth general elections in 1967 when the Swatantra–Jana Congress government was formed with R.N. Singh Deo, the Swatantra Party leader, as Chief Minister. Split in the Congress in 1969 and the consequent changes in the relations between the Congress party of Orissa and the Jana Congress led to withdrawal of the Jana Congress from the Ministry in January 1971.

The Assembly elections held in 1971 left the situation equally fluid although the Congress(I) emerged as the largest party. But a government could be formed by a coalition of the Swatantra Party and the Utkal Congress and supported by the Jharkhand Party. The Ministry was headed by Biswanth Das, a veteran Congressman who returned from political retirement. But the Ministry broke down barely after 14 months, with the defection of some Swatantra members and the merger of the Utkal Congress with the Congress (I). Thereafter the State had a long spell of Congress rule, with a brief Janata interrugnum between 1978-80 and a Janata Dal government under Biju Patnaik until it was replaced by the fourth coalition government of Biju Janata Dal and the BJP elected in the Assembly elections of February 2000.

None of the first three coalition governments could complete a full term, and they broke down owing to intra-coalition conflicts or factional infighting within the constituents. The fourth government led by the Biju Janata Dal (BJD) and headed by Naveen Patnaik is cemented by the common interests of the BJP and the BJD who are also partners in the Central government and therefore depend on mutual support at the Centre and in the State.

The political situation in Uttar Pradesh was slightly different from that of the other States after the fourth general election. The Congress emerged as the largest party in the Legislative Assembly but it failed to secure absolute majority. However, the Congress managed to form a government of its own under C.B. Gupta as Chief Minister with the support of seventeen independent MLAs and four other MLAs who joined the Congress. But soon dissensions broke out in the Congress and Charan Singh, together with sixteen followers, left the Congress to form his own party, the Jana Congress. At the time of voting on the motion of thanks to the Governor's address, the Jana Congress voted with the opposition and defeated the government. On resignation of C.B. Gupta's Ministry, Charan Singh was elected leader of the opposition United Front and was sworn in as Chief Minister on 3 April, 1967.[6] However the government could not function smoothly, and MLAs started leaving the UF fold in batches until Charan Singh tendered his resignation on 17 February, 1968. The State was placed under President's rule and the Assembly dissolved.

Fresh elections were held on 9 February, 1969, and the Congress having secured majority in the Assembly, C.B. Gupta again formed the government on 26 February, 1969. Following the split in the Congress at the national level in 1969, some Congress MLAs led by Kamalapathi Tripathi left the Congress. Possibilities of a coalition government were explored but differences could not be settled regarding who was to lead a new government. After days of "bargaining games", Charan Singh who had by this time merged the Jana Congress with the Bharatiya Kranti Dal formed the second coalition government together with the Congress (I) on 17 February, 1970. The BKD soon fell out with the Congress (I) on several issues including nationalization of sugar mills in the State and the abolition of privy purse by the Centre. The situation reached a breaking point when the Chief Minister asked thirteen out of twenty-six Congress ministers to resign and the latter refused. The Chief Minister then requested the Governor to dismiss the ministers, and the Congress in a countermove withdrew support and demanded the dismissal of the government. Although the Congress (O), Jan Sangh, Swatantra and Samyukta Socialist Party decided to extend support to the Charan Singh Ministry, the Governor recommended suspension of the Assembly and the proclamation of President's rule. And thus the second coalition came to an end on 1 October, 1970.

On the same day, the Congress (O), Jan Sangh and Swatantra Party agreed to form a United Legislative Party (Samyukta Vidhayak Dal) which was joined by the BKD in four days. The SVD thus came to have a strength of 242 members in a House of 425, and elected T.N. Singh of the Congress (O) as their leader. After seventeen days of the President's rule, the SVD coalition under T.N. Singh came to power. As T.N. Singh was not a member of the legislature he sought election on 5 January, 1971 but was defeated by a Congress (I) candidate. However he continued as Chief Minister until 30 March, 1971 when he tendered his resignation on the passage of an amendment to the official motion of thanks to the Governor. Several single-party Congress governments followed, with a Janata interregnum after the Emergency (1975-77). All political developments in UP were pushed under the carpet of history and politics stood still during the long spell of President's rule lasting from 1985 to 1997. The second phase of coalition politics in UP appeared when the elections were held in March 1997. The party position in the UP Legislative Assembly in 1997 was as follows:

Bharatiya Janata Party	–	175
Bahujan Samaj Party	–	67
Samajwadi Party	–	110
Congress (I)	–	37
Bharatiya Kisan Kamgar Party	–	8
Janata Dal	–	7
CPI	–	1
CPI (M)	–	4
Samata Party	–	2
Samajwadi Janata Party	–	1
Independents	–	13
Total seats	–	425[7]

The President's rule continued until 21 March, 1997. Through a protracted process of discussions a novel political formula was devised between the BSP and the BJP to co-operate in spite of their being bitter enemies in the election. According to the formula the Chief Ministership was to rotate between coalition partners — BJP and BSP — after every six months. The working of the Ministry was to be monitored by a three-member panel comprising Vajpayee, Advani and Kanshi Ram. The first term of Chief Ministership was to be with the BSP and Speakership with the BJP. It was also agreed that the political situation would be reviewed by the two parties at the end of one year.

The Ministry did not work smoothly, and a serious friction arose on the question of the change of Chief Minister and Speaker at the end of the first term of six months. However it was decided to retain the Speakership with the BJP, and Kalyan Singh of BJP was sworn in as Chief Minister on 21 September 1997. The friction continued and the BSP pulled out of the government within a month. An unusual spectacle of horse-trading and defection followed which helped prop up the Kalyan Singh Ministry in power. Twenty-two out of thirty-seven Congress (I) MLAs formed the Loktantrik Congress Party and three out of seven Janata Dal members formed a separate group. Twelve rebel BSP members also joined the pro-Kalyan Singh camp. All defectors were rewarded with ministerships, raising the total number of ministers to 93 — the biggest ever Ministry in the Indian States. Although BJP could strengthen its hold on the government with artificial support encouraging defection in the opposition ranks, Chief Ministers had to be shifted to accommodate intra-coalitional conflicts and BJP's factional infighting.[8]

Uttar Pradesh has thus experimented with coalition governments, but governmental stability has been always undermined by the ulterior motives of power-mongering politicians. The trends established in the earlier phases are still maintained, resulting in frequent changes of ministries and their unscrupulous expansion. No serious efforts have been made to forge pre-poll alliances with any commitment to a common agenda; even the present ruling coalition is a post-poll, hotchpotch arrangement. No institutional mechanism has been created to effectively co-ordinate the coalition partners or iron out their differences.

The State of Haryana, born on 1 November, 1966 out of the reorganisation of the State of Punjab, has been notorious for the defection games of its politicians. At the time of its formation the Congress party was able to make a government of its own under Bhagwat Dayal Sharma as Chief Minister who was reappointed as such after the Assembly elections of 1967.[9] But differences arose within the Congress on the question of Ministry formation, and the dissidents formed a new party — the Haryana Congress — and elected Rao Birendra Singh as its leader. The opposition parties collaborated with the Haryana Congress to form the United Front and elected Birendra Singh as the United Front leader. The latter was sworn in as the first coalition Chief Minister on 24 March, 1967. But as a result of frequent floor-crossings the relative strength of parties underwent changes and the Governor was compelled to dismiss the Ministry on 21 November, 1967 and bring about President's rule in the State.

In the mid-term elections of May 1968, the Congress secured absolute majority and Bansi Lal became the Congress Chief Minister. But the game of defections continued and obstructed the functioning of the Legislative Assembly. Ultimately on the recommendation of the Chief Minister, the Governor dissolved the Assembly on 21 January, 1972. After the next elections held within three months, the Congress (I) could provide a single-party government which completed the full term. In the 1977 elections, the Janata party secured absolute majority and formed a single-party government. However, after the Congress victory in the Lok Sabha polls in 1980, it was not found necessary to dissolve the Haryana Assembly as the Chief Minister Bhajan Lal had moved to the Congress camp with enough followers and could ensure a full term. The 1982 Assembly elections resulted in a fragmented situation wherein no party had enough majority to form a government.[10] The Congress (I) and the Lok Dal-BJP combine staked their claims, and the Governor invited the Congress (I) leader Bhajan Lal to form the government. Bhajan Lal could complete the term without much interruption with the support of independents and defectors from the Lok Dal.

The second coalition Ministry in Haryana came to office after the elections of June 1987 in which the Lok Dal (Bahuguna group) and its electoral ally BJP made a clean sweep.[11] Lok Dal had enough strength to form its own government, but Devi Lal who became Chief Minister included some BJP members also in the Ministry. Instability of government continued to haunt Haryana from 1987 to 1991 when there were seven governments under five Chief Ministers. The next major coalitional development took place after the 1996 Assembly elections in which the BJP was an ally of the Haryana Vikas Party (HVP) led by Bansi Lal. A coalition government of the two parties was formed under Bansi Lal as Chief Minister. Inter-party conflict led to the withdrawal of support by BJP which rendered the government in a minority. Although the Congress (I) offered to prop up the HVP Ministry, they had to back out as Bansi Lal did not accede to some of their conditions.[12] Further a section of the HVP legislators broke away and helped the Indian National Lok Dal under Om Prakash Chautala to form a government in July 1999. In the February 2000 Assembly elections, held one year and a half ahead of schedule, the INLD fought in alliance with the BJP under the NDA banner and secured 47 and 6 seats respectively in an Assembly of 90 members in total. Although there are several points of conflict between the INLD and the BJP at the State level as well as at the national level, the alliance continues as a coalition government even after the elections.

Another major State where coalition government exists today is Maharashtra. In the Assembly elections held in September-October 1999 no party or combine could secure absolute majority. The BJP-Shiv Sena alliance which was ruling the State at this time was short of 20 seats to reach majority (Shiv Sena-69, BJP-56) in a House of 288.[13] The Congress (I) emerged as the largest party with 75 seats and the National Congress Party secured 58. The Congress (I) and the NCP had fought the elections independently and were enemies, the latter having broken away from the Congress (I) on the eve of the elections. However, after hard negotiations the Congress (I) and the NCP agreed to work together and form a coalition with the help of minor parties like the Peasants and Workers Party, Janata Dal (Secular), Samajwadi Party, Republican Party of India,

Bahujan Mahasangh and the CPI(M). The new coalition Ministry took office towards the end of October 1999 under Vilasrao Deshmukh of Congress(I) as Chief Minister and Chhagan Bhujbal of NCP as Deputy Chief Minister.

The first coalition government of Maharashtra, formed by BJP and Shiv Sena, which ruled the State since 1995 had begun rather smoothly. But they developed intra-coalition conflicts and factional infights within the Shiv Sena, leading to the replacement of the Chief Minister Manohar Joshi by Narayan Rane, both belonging to the Shiv Sena.[14] The present coalition includes two major partners who cannot be normally expected to work together, being factions of the same party and bitter fighters in the last election. But the attractions of power on the one hand and the alternative of losing it to a communal combine on the other forced the two secular parties — Congress(I) and NCP — to forge a post-poll coalition.

On the whole, out of the 28 States in India as on 1 January, 2001, 15 States have coalition governments and 12 single-party governments.

State-wise breakdown

States with Congress (I) Governments	States with BJP governments	Other single-party governments
1. Arunachal Pradesh	1. Gujarat	1. Andhra Pradesh
2. Chattisgarh		2. Assam
3. Karnataka		3. Jammu & Kashmir
4. Madhya Pradesh		4. Sikkim
5. Nagaland		5. Tamil Nadu
6. Rajastan		

States with Congress (I) led Coalitions	States with BJP-led Coalitions	Other coalitions
1. Maharashtra	1. Goa	1. Bihar
	2. Himachal Pradesh	2. Haryana
	3. Jharkhand	3. Kerala
	4. Uttaranchal	4. Meghalaya
	5. Uttar Pradesh	5. Mizoram
		6. Orissa
		7. Punjab
		8. West Bengal
		9. Tripura

Having been formed by the combination of different variables and sub-variables, each coalition may have different characteristics. Based on an analysis of sub-variables, Iqbal Narain drew up a typology of coalition governments that existed in 1967.[15]

Coalitional Types by Sub-variables

1.	By time sequence of coalition formation : pre-election or post-election	1. (a)	Electoral alliance-turned governmental coalition
		(b)	Post-election governmental coalition
2.	By mutual strength of coalition partners	2. (a)	One-party dominant governmental coalition
		(b)	Major-party dominant governmental coalition
3.	By strength of coalition partners *vis-à-vis* legislative strength	3. (a)	Majority governmental coalition
		(b)	Minority governmental coalition
4.	By ideological orientation of coalition partner	4. (a)	Ideologically homogeneous governmental coalition
		(b)	Ideologically heterogeneous governmental coalition
		(a)	Leftist governmental coalition
		(c)	Rightist governmental coalition
		(d)	Centrist governmental coalition
		(e)	Ideologically neutral governmental coalition
5.	By number of coalition partners	5. (a)	Many party governmental coalition
		(b)	Two-party governmental coalition
		(c)	Few-party governmental coalition
6.	By interaction of infrastructure and politics	6. (a)	Infrastructure dominated coalition
		(b)	Secular coalition

Based on the movement of coalitional politics through several stages of development, Iqbal Naṛain makes another categorisation[16]:

(i) the phase of anti-Congress non-ideological coalition politics (1967-69);

(ii) the phase of anti-Congress programmatic coalitional politics (1969) from mid-term poll to the Congress split; and

(iii) the phase of politico-programmatic coalitional politics (1969-70) from the Congress split and after.

Jawaharlal Pandey has made a slight modification on Iqbal Narain's three-phased category in his analysis of Bihar politics by increasing the number to five[17] :

(i) the phase of anti-Congress non-ideological coalitional politics;

(ii) the phase of anti-Congress ideological coalitional politics;

(iii) the phase of anti-non-Congress coalitional politics;

(iv) the phase of anti-Congress programmatic coalitional politics; and

(v) the phase of opportunistic coalitional politics.

As all the above phases are not applicable to all States in the country a more comprehensive and generally applicable phase-based categorisation may be adopted as : (i) experimental phase; (ii) opportunistic phase; and (iii) stability phase. In every State's coalitional politics, political stability is finally achieved by passing through the earlier phases, whether prolonged or short. If the power game is well motivated and meant finally to achieve political stability, the opportunistic phase in which coalition partners use their clout for political bargaining may be viewed from a more sympathetic and more academic perspective. Opportunism and floor-crossing, in such a perspective, become strategies of identify-search, provided the political process ultimately results in polarisation and stability. The model is Kerala where a bipolarization has developed between the LDF alliance and the UDF alliance leading to political stability. However the political stability thus achieved need not necessarily be a permanent phenomenon inasmuch as a single-party stability cannot also be a permanent one.

Out of the fifteen States with coalition governments a few have achieved political stability through continuous experimentation and methodical practice on the part of the political parties and leaders (Kerala and West Bengal). A second category consists of States that have moved back and forth between one-party government and coalition without having the opportunity to practise coalition politics with commitment (Uttar Pradesh, Bihar and Goa). A third category manages coalitions under the patronage of anchor parties, i.e. one party having enough strength to run the government but willing to share some power with the poll allies (Haryana, Orissa, Punjab and West Bengal). The fourth category includes new entrants, still in the experimental stage (Maharashtra).

The fourth general election (1967) was believed to have marked a watershed in Indian politics, as it broke the Congress dominance in several States and aroused hopes of political polarization.[18] But later developments resulted in the further fragmentation of party structure and gave rise to a more competitive multi-polar politics. The emergence of new political parties and forces including the regional parties occurred at the expense of the dominant Congress which was cut down to size in several States and subsequently at the Centre. Not only are the regional parties today cutting at the roots of the Congress power they are also checking the growth of any alternative party including the BJP at the national level. The two NDA experiments at the Centre seem to strengthen the view that there is no going back to single-party dominance of any complexion -- secular or non-secular, socialist or non-socialist.

NOTES

1. Dalip Singh, *Dynamics of Punjab Politics*, Macmillan (New Delhi, 1981), p. 93.
2. S.K. Khanna, *Coalition Politics in India*, Commonwealth Publishers (New Delhi, 1999), p. 26.
3. Jawaharlal Pandey, *State Politics In India,*Uppal (New Delhi, 1982), p. 14.
4. *Outlook,* 20 March 2000, p. 24.
5. R.N. Mishra, "Patterns of Coalitional Politics in Orissa", in A.A. Padhi (ed), *Indian State Politics: A Case Study of Orissa,* BR Publishing Corporation (Delhi, 1985), pp. 74-76.
6. S.K. Khanna, n (2), p. 39.
7. *Diary of Political Events, (*1997), Lok Sabha Secretariat.

8. Kalyan Singh was replaced by R.P. Gupta and later by Rajnath Singh, both of the BJP, as Chief Minister. Kalyan Singh organised another party after his suspension from the BJP.
9. Bhagwat Dayal Sharma assumed office on 10 March, 1967 and had to resign within two weeks.
10. The result was as follows: Congress (I)–36; Lok Dal–31; BJP–6; JNP–1; Independents and others–12.
11. The election results: Lok Dal (B)–58; BJP–15; Cong. (I)–5;, CPI–1; CPI (M)–1; Independents–6
12. T.R. Rajalakshmi, "Chautala Rides on", *Frontline,* 17 March 2000, p.17.
13. *The Hindu* (Thiruvananthapuram), 10 October 1999.
14. *Ibid.* 31 January 1999.
15. Iqbal Narain, "Constitutional Politics in India and the Political System: The Crisis of Compatibility", reprinted in D. Sunder Ram (ed), *Indian Parliamentary Opposition*, Kanishka (New Delhi, 1996), p. 195.
16. Cited in Jawaharlal Pandey, n. (3), p. 29.
17. *Ibid.*, p. 29.
18. *Ibid.*, p. 40.

3

COALITION POLITICS AT THE CENTRE

This chapter traces the evolution of coalition politics at the national level since 1977. Although coalition politics of any significance started with the Janata experiment a genuine coalition government could install itself in power at the Centre only with the United Front Government of 1996. This chapter analyses in detail the problems of Cabinet formation and Cabinet management under various coalitions from 1996 to the end of 2000.

The Janata Experiment

Coalition experiment at the Centre can be traced to the first non-Congress government led by the Janata party (1977-80). The Janata party was the offspring of the continuous struggles made by the opposition parties to pull down the Congress from power. Frustrated by the authoritarianism of the Congress during the Emergency (1975-77), certain opposition parties and groups decided to fight the next general elections under a common banner and thus provide an alternative to the Congress. On the initiative given by Jayaprakash Narayan who provided moral leadership to Indian politics at the time, the Congress (O), the Jan Sangh, the Socialist party and the Bharatiya Lok Dal came together to undertake the challenge.

On 20 January 1977, the leaders of the above parties met in Delhi to chalk out their strategy for the elections. As the first step, this development was to have a tremendous impact on Indian politics. They decided to fight the Lok Sabha elections unitedly under one flag and with one programme. Morarji Desai who became leader of the party announced the decision to go to the polls under the name of the Janata party. An executive committee was set-up to monitor the selection of candidates, drafting of the election manifesto and management of the party's election campaign. The Swatantra party became its constituent on 24 January, 1977.

It was at this time that Jagjivan Ram, H.N. Bahuguna, Nandini Satpathy and others resigned from the Congress party and announced the formation of the Congress For Democracy (CFD). This group joined the Janata party as an ally. The Janata and the CFD mobilised all anti-Emergency forces in the country and ensured the election of a non-Congress government for the first time at the Centre. Although lacking in resources and organisational machinery the Janata had leaders of rich political acumen, led by Jayaprakash Narayan who had the moral halo of a national leader almost of Nehruvian stature.

The general elections were held during March 1977, and the non-Congress opposition could sweep the polls. The sixth Lok Sabha gave surprise to the country by defeating the Congress as well as its leader Mrs. Gandhi at the hustings.

The Janata party secured 271 and the CFD 28 seats respectively.[1] Among the Janata party constituents, the breakdown was as follows: Bharatiya Jan Sangh – 93, Bharatiya Lok Dal – 71; Congress (O) – 51; Socialists – 28; Chandrasekhar Group – 6 and others – 25. The formal Constitution of the Janata by merging the constituents took place only on 1 May, 1977, i.e. after the formation of the government, although the constituent groups were fighting the elections with a common symbol — the symbol of Haldhar — previously allotted to the Bharatiya Lok Dal (BLD).

The disparate nature of the Janata asserted itself when the party was faced with the task of electing its leader who was to take over the role of the Prime Minister. Jagjivan Ram of CFD, Charan Singh of BLD and Morarji Desai of Congress (O) were serious contenders for the post. When Morarji Desai was elected leader and was sworn in as Prime Minister on 24 March, 1977, the other two felt betrayed. And factionalism continued even after the formation of the government.

The decision of the Janata government to dissolve the nine Congress-ruled State governments and hold fresh elections aggravated the infighting. The distribution of tickets for State Assembly seats added fuel to the fire. Seven States — UP, Bihar,

Rajasthan, MP, Orissa, Haryana and Himachal Pradesh — were won by the Janata party in the elections of June 1977, and the Chief Ministerships were shared by the two constituents — the BJS and the BLD. The other constituents were disappointed. In the Assembly elections that followed in February 1978 in the States of Andhra Pradesh, Karnataka, Maharashtra, Assam and Meghalaya, the Congress party made an impressive victory in the first three States. This gave further occasion for bitter criticism of the party president Chandrasekhar by Charan Singh and Raj Narain. Charan Singh had in fact opposed the election of Chandrasekhar as president of the party.

After a few months reconciliation was reached in the party with the decision to have two Deputy Prime Ministers. Charan Singh and Jagjivan Ram were installed as Deputy Prime Ministers. However, Charan Singh's faction continued to be active within the party and was routed in the parliamentary party elections in May 1979.[2] All the six important posts in the parliamentary party were won by an informal alliance of the BJS and the Congress (O) groups. Charan Singh continued to entertain hopes about becoming the Prime Minister and Raj Narain, a socialist and Charan Singh's close associate, used every opportunity to press for the same. Although it was Raj Narain who was responsible for the Allahabad High Court judgement against Mrs. Gandhi which eventually forced her to declare the Emergency, he was compelled to seek her help and advice to overthrow Moarji Desai.[3] Raj Narain was removed from the national executive of the party for one year for his personal attack on party leaders and open criticism of government policies. Protesting against the decision and alleging RSS domination in the party, he resigned from the party and formed the Janata (Secular). It was in these circumstances that the Congress party had brought a no-confidence motion against Morarji Ministry and got it passed. On 15 July, 1979 Morarji Desai submitted his resignation.[4] Following the Ministry's fall Charan Singh left the party and formed a separate Janata (J) party. Bahuguna, S.N. Misra and others also deserted the Janata party.

Y.B. Chavan, the leader of the Congress parliamentary party, was then called by President N. Sanjeeva Reddy to form the government. Being unable to secure a majority, the Congress declined the offer. The President then invited Charan Singh who felt confident of getting external support from the Congress. Charan Singh was asked to prove his majority in the House at the earliest possible opportunity within three weeks' time. On 20 August, 1979, he submitted his resignation without even moving the confidence motion, having failed to ensure the support of the Congress. On 22 August, 1979 the President dissolved the Lok Sabha and ordered fresh elections. Charan Singh government continued as caretaker.

In the elections held in January 1980, to constitute the seventh Lok Sabha, the Congress (I) led by Mrs. Gandhi secured a two-third majority and the Janata constituents were reduced to small proportions. Thus the dream of providing a durable alternative government was shattered by the sudden collapse of the party. The Janata was not able to attain the cohesion and unity required of a single party. The only uniting factor was perhaps the nomenclature, the members being loyal to former groups to which they once belonged. The power-hungry Janata leaders were indulging in mutual bickering and mud slinging which made the government congenitally unstable. Lack of discipline among party leaders led to disobedience of the party high command and public criticism of governmental policies. Finally, there was no ideological homogeneity among the constituent parties which joined together to provide an alternative to the Congress (I).[5]

The Janata experiment came to a close with the disintegration of the party thereafter. It was neither a single party government nor a coalition government. Having had their experience and training in the single-party dominance system of the Congress, the leaders failed to imagine how to develop a consensus or coalition system among the different political groups that comprised the Janata. Eyeing each other with suspicion, the constituent parties forgot their competition with the Congress and indulged in conflict among themselves. Further their policy during the regime appeared to be retributive action against Mrs. Gandhi rather than any positive programme of action to rectify the errors of the previous Congress governments.

The National Front Government

The next serious attempt to form a non-Congress government at the Centre was made in 1988 by a coalition of parties called the National Front under the leadership of V.P Singh, the Defence Minister in Rajiv Gandhi's Cabinet who had resigned in protest. The seven-party National Front formally launched on 17 September, 1988 consisted of a conglomeration of ideologically disparate, regionally based political parties and groups committed to ousting the Congress from power. The seven parties included: the Jan Morcha, the Janata party, the Lok Dal, the Congress(S), the Telugu Desam, the Dravida Munnetra Kazhagom and the Assam Gana Parishad. The new found unity was the result of the continuous efforts on the part of V.P. Singh and of N.T. Rama Rao, the Telugu Desam leader and Chief Minister of Andhra Pradesh.

V.P. Singh, after his resignation from the Rajiv Gandhi Cabinet and subsequent suspension from the Congress(I), carried on a campaign against corruption in high levels and formed the Jan Morcha as a forum to voice his views. The Jan Morcha was welcomed by other groups and politicians opposed to the Congress (I) who volunteered to share platforms with V.P. Singh and oraganise joint campaigns to root out corruption and tackle other pressing problems facing the people.[6] This sense of cooperation among the opposition parties led to the formation of a common national platform for the Jan Morcha, the Janata party, the Congress (S) and the Lok Dal (A) led by Ajit Singh. A joint statement issued at New Delhi by the group listed fourteen issues which might constitute the core of the strategy to give the country an alternative policy, a new social order and a better tomorrow.[7] The list included electoral reforms, decentralisation of political and economic power, elimination of corruption at all levels and a self-reliant economy with rural parity. Addressing a rally in Bangalore tc mark five years of Janata rule in Karnataka, several non-Congress (I) Chief Ministers and opposition leaders affirmed the need for forming an effective anti-Congress (I) front. The rally was addressed by several opposition leaders including the Chief Ministers of Andhra Pradesh, Assam, Haryana, Karnataka and West Bengal.[8] A series of joint rallies and conferences culminated in the merger of Lok Dal(A) and Rashtriya Sanjay Manch into the Janata party.[9] There were similar moves for bringing together other opposition parties at that time. The opposition moves got an impetus from the election of V.P. Singh from Allahabad Lok Sabha constituency in the by-elections held in June 1988 with a margin of 110,000 votes. Further, this made V.P. Singh the undisputed leader of the opposition parties, relegating the claims of other aspirants like Chandrasekhar and Devi Lal into the background.

Efforts to merge like-minded parties such as the Janata, Lok Dal, Congress (S) and Jan Morcha continued without apparent success. The main hindrance appeared to be the personal jealousies and ambitions of the leaders of these parties. After much dillydallying, the Janata party, Jan Morcha and the Devi Lal faction of Lok Dal merged and finally launched the Janata Dal on 11 October, 1988.[10] The Congress (S) and the Bahuguna faction of Lok Dal remained aloof. The birth of Janata Dal was acclaimed as a turning point in Indian politics as it promised a centrist, secular alternative to the Congress. The new party was recognised by the Speaker on the floor of the Lok Sabha in April 1989 and was also recognised as a national party by the Election Commission of India in October 1989. Nevertheless personal enmities remained between leaders like V.P. Singh, Chandrasekhar, Devi Lal, Bahuguna, Ajit Singh and others.[11]

Simultaneously, parallel moves were being made under the leadership of N.T. Rama Rao to forge unity in the opposition ranks. This resulted in the formation of the National Front on 17 September, 1988 — about three weeks before the formation of the Janata Dal. That is to say, the formation of the National Front preceded the formation of the Janata Dal. Of the seven member parties of the National Front, the Janata, the Jan Morcha and the Lok Dal joined to form the Janata Dal; the other four parties preferred to retain their identity. Thus the number of National Front constituents was reduced to five: the Janata Dal, the Congress (S), the AGP, the DMK and the TDP. N.T. Rama Rao was made Chairman of the National Front.

The leaders of the Front turned to the right and left quarters for support. Rama Rao held discussions with Jyoti Basu while V.P. Singh and others shared platforms with the BJP. But the ideological difference between the CPI and CPI (M) groups on the one hand and the BJP on the other stood in the way of opposition unity moves in the first half of 1989 election year. The second half of the year witnessed a change in the attitude of the political parties. The opposition parties realised that the Congress (I) was at its weakest and their failure to grasp the situation would never be forgiven by the people. In June 1989, the BJP President L.K. Advani announced the party consensus on the question of seat adjustment with the Janata Dal and other constituents of the National Front in the Lok Sabha elections.[12] After two more days the national conference of RSP held in New Delhi decided to have electoral alliance with National Front to avoid division of votes.

On 17 October, 1989 the Election Commission announced the schedule of the 9th general elections to be held on 22 and 24 November, 1989. The election proclamation brought about the occasion for a rare display of unity among the opposition parties. Seat adjustment talks with the BJP and the left parties got under way. The Election Commission recognised eight political parties as national parties with reserved symbols for the coming Lok Sabha and Assembly elections.[13] They were: the Congress (I), Janata Dal, the Lok Dal (B), the Janata Party, the BJP, the CPI, the CPI (M) and the Congress (S).

In these circumstances the BJP softened its stand towards the Janata Dal and the National Front. The left parties too agreed to make seat adjustments with parties allied to the BJP. It was clear that the old reservations had to be shed under compulsions of realpolitik. It was publicly claimed that the Janata Dal had made no open alliance with either the BJP or the Communists; but in fact their State units were permitted to make electoral adjustments with both.[14]

In the 9th general election that followed, the Congress (I) won the largest number of seats but had no majority to form the government. The Congress (I) made it known that they had no intention to stake the claim for forming a government. So the opposition parties started their moves. The National Front presidium met in New Delhi and constituted a five-member committee to initiate talks with non-Congress (I) parties.[15] The members of the committee were: N.T. Rama Rao, V.P. Singh,

Devi Lal, Ajit Singh and Arun Nehru. The committee members held discussions with representatives of BJP and the left parties. As a result, the CPI, CPI(M), RSP and the Forward Bloc decided to extend unconditional support from outside to the National Front to form a government.[16] The BJP also offered to give "general but critical support" to the National Front to run a minority government without participating in it.[17] Meanwhile, an attempt was made to explore the possibility of forming a government of "national reconciliation" by including all national political parties, but the idea was not acceptable to all parties and leaders.

Table 3.1 : Seats Won by Various Parties in the 1989 Lok Sabha Election

Congress (I)	197
Janata Dal	143
Baratiya Janata Party	85
Janata Party	0
Lok Kranti Dal	0
Communist Party of India	12
Communist Party of India (Marxist)	33
ICSS	1
Telugu Desam Party	2
Dravida Munnetra Kazhagom	0
Other major State parties	22
Others	22
Independents	12
Total	**529**

The Janata Dal parliamentary party meeting, presided over by Madhu Dandavate, elected V.P. Singh as its leader. Although V.P. Singh was popularly thought of as the Prime Ministerial candidate, Devi Lal and Chandrasekhar were strong aspirants and were trying every means to subvert the election of V.P. Singh as the parliamentary leader. It was by prolonged persuasion and pressure that the two leaders were made to accept the election of V.P. Singh as the leader. V.P. Singh proposed Devi Lal as the leader of the parliamentary party and Chandrasekhar seconded it. But Devi Lal declined and proposed the name of V.P. Singh, and Ajit Singh seconded the proposal. The drama gave tense moments as there was a general fear about

Devi Lal's changing moods. Madhu Dandavate then declared V.P. Singh elected as the leader of Janata Dal parliamentary party. Chandrasekhar, however, expressed his reservation about the manner in which the election was conducted.[18] Then the National Front parliamentary party also elected V.P. Singh as its leader unanimously.[19]

The President of India, R. Venkataraman, invited Rajiv Gandhi to form the government following the principle of first invitation to the largest party. When he declined, having had no majority for his party and having no intention to seek support from other parties, Venkataraman turned to V.P. Singh, the leader of the second largest party, the Janata Dal. The President stipulated that V.P. Singh would have to "take a vote of confidence in the Lok Sabha within thirty days of his assuming office", which he did successfully with the help of the BJP and the Communists. The National Front was supposed to be a wider forum comprising five national and regional parties; but the Janata Dal alone had 143 members out of 146 of the National Front. Hence the National Front was not in fact a coalition, and the National Front government was a minority government led by the Janata Dal and supported by the BJP and the left parties without participating in the government. Nor did the Front parties have a common minimum programme to unite themselves and the ideologically distant supporting parties. The Front leaders did not think of evolving any mechanism for the effective co-ordination and monitoring of the government, not to speak of nurturing a new political culture.

The natural and inherent differences in the National Front government came to surface within a short time of its formation. In August 1990, the V.P. Singh government, following its own electoral calculations, decided to implement the recommendations of the Mandal Commission report under which 52 per cent of the government jobs had to be reserved for the Scheduled Castes and Other Backward Castes. The government took the decision without consulting the supporting parties. The decision antagonised the BJP as such a move would adversely affect the electoral interests of the party. V.P. Singh's decision was highly unpopular among the urban upper caste and middle class Hindus who served as BJP's vote bank. Further the arrest of L.K. Advani in Bihar, during the course of his Ayodhya-linked *Ratha Yatra,* by the Janata Dal government of the State gave impetus to BJP's decision to withdraw support to the National Front government. On withdrawal of support by the BJP, the President asked V.P. Singh to prove his majority in the Lok Sabha. The eleven-month-old minority government of V.P. Singh was voted out of power on 7 November 1990 with passing of a no-confidence motion in the Lok Sabha with 346 votes against the Government and 142 in favour.

The threat to the National Front government came not merely from the external supporters, but also from within. The Janata Dal was not fully integrated in spite of the merger of the Janata party, Lok Dal and Jan Morcha. Factions of the Janata Dal and Lok Dal had remained separate, protesting against the policy of the official leadership. And the factions that merged (led by leaders like Chandrasekhar and Devi Lal) were unhappy about the dominance of the Jan Morcha and its leader V.P. Singh. This unhappiness manifested itself when the Janata Dal broke up under their leaders into new political outfits.

After the fall of V.P. Singh government on 7 November, 1990, the Janata Dal was split by Chandrasekhar who with the support of 55 members formed the Janata Dal (Samajwadi). Chandrasekhar assumed the office of Prime Minister on 10 November, 1990 with the support of the Congress (I). This was another minority government, not a coalition, solely dependent on the outside support of the Congress and was bound to repeat the fate of the earlier minority government led by Charan Singh. President R. Venkataraman is reported to have enquired whether the Congress support would last for at least one year. Rajiv Gandhi replied: "Why one year? It could continue to the life of the Lok Sabha."[20] Differences occurred soon between the government and the Congress(I) on various issues relating to Punjab, Kashmir and Assam, the economy of the country, rising prices and the question of permitting US planes to refuel in India.[21] Finally, came the allegation from the Congress (I) that its President Rajiv Gandhi's residence at 10 Janpath, New Delhi was being kept under the constant surveillance of Haryana intelligence men. The Congress (I) walk-out in the Lok Sabha on this issue led to adjournment of the House twice for want of quorum. The Congress party's decision to stay out from the House until adequate action was taken against all concerned forced Chandrasekhar to submit his resignation on 6 March, 1991 and advise the President to dissolve the Lok Sabha. The President of India, R. Venkataraman, dissolved the ninth Lok Sabha on 13 March, 1991 and ordered fresh elections. Chandrasekhar continued as caretaker Prime Minister.

In the next elections held in May-June 1991, the Congress(I) emerged as the largest single party with 224 seats, but without majority. Being the leader of the largest party, P.V. Narasimha Rao formed the government and surprisingly he could complete the five-year term.

The United Front Government

The eleventh Lok Sabha elected in April-May 1996 witnessed a severely fractured verdict with no one party or alliance being able to come anywhere near an absolute majority. It was a multi-cornered fight, the BJP alone being able to give the semblance of an alliance. The Congress fought it alone with perhaps some electoral adjustments at the State level. The National Front (NF) and Left Front (LF) parties could not reach any agreement about a third front as a viable alternative to the Congress and the BJP. Despite several rounds of talks, neither the NF nor the LF could agree on their allies or on a common programme. The main cause was the absence of any strong focal point or a leader who could bring them together. The greatest obstacles arose at the State level, particularly in UP, AP and Tamil Nadu where the State unit leaders could not agree to work with their rivals.[22]

The BJP emerged as the single largest party with 160 seats as against 139 seats won by the Congress(I). Atal Behari Vajpayee was unanimously elected leader of the BJP parliamentary party. A delegation led by L.K. Advani met the President of India to stake claim to form the next government.[23]

Meanwhile the Samata party national executive decided to give issue-based support to the BJP and requested the President to invite the BJP leader to form the government. The President Shanker Dayal Sharma invited Vajpayee on 15 May, 1996 to form the government and asked him to prove his majority on the floor of Lok Sabha by 31 May, 1996.

Table 3.2 : Seats Won by Various Parties in the 1996 Lok Sabha Elections[24]

Total Seats – 543

BJP and allies			**Congress and allies**		**NF-LF and others**		
BJP	-	160	Congress (I)	139	Janata Dal	-	45
Shiv Sena	-	15			CPI (M)	-	32
Samata	-	8			CPI	-	12
Haryana Vikas party	-	3			FB	-	3
	-	**186**			RSP	-	5
					SP	-	17
					BSP	-	11
					DMK	-	17
					TMC	-	20
					TDP	-	16
					Akali Dal	-	8
					AGP	-	5
					AICC (T)	-	5
					Others	-	19
						-	**215**

At this time the National Front and the Left Front parties were working hard to forge unity among themselves to stake claim to form the government as well as to check the BJP from reaching power. The Congress (I) Working Committee also decided on 13 May, 1996 to ensure that the BJP would not be able to form the government.[25] In a pre-emptive strike, the NF-LF combine elected H.D. Deve Gowda, the Janata Dal Chief Minister of Karnataka on 13, May 1996 as their candidate for Premiership, and the election was communicated to the President. The election of Deve Gowda was made after a process of elimination, with V.P. Singh, Jyoti Basu and G.K. Moopanar declining to take the responsibility. Jyoti Basu was in fact willing to become the Prime Minister, but the party politbureau decided otherwise. Still it was surprising that the claims of better known politicians like Ramakrishna Hegde were ignored. The leaders who supported Gowda and signed the communication to the President were: H.S. Surjeet (CPI-M), Indrajit Gupta (CPI), Laloo Prasad Yadav (JD), M. Karunanidhi (DMK), G.K. Moopanar (TMC), Mulayam Singh Yadav (SP), Chandrababu Naidu (TDP), Durgadas Boro (AGP), Madhav Rao Scindia (MVPC) and N.D. Tiwari (Cong-

T).[26] Deve Gowda now formally requested the Congress (I) to extend their support to the Third Front in the formation of government. However, the President summoned Vajpayee on 15 May to the discomfiture of the Third Front who criticised the Presidential action as "hasty".

Thus the first BJP Prime Minister was sworn in on 16 May, 1996 along with eleven Cabinet Ministers. But Vajpayee could not settle down to office as he had to muster enough support to keep up the Ministry. Nor could the Third Front leaders, they being committed to snatching away power from the BJP.

The NF-LF leaders now renamed the Third Front as the United Front (UF) and formally elected Deve Gowda the leader of the United Front parliamentary party. The United Front consisted of nine parties of the National Front (JD, TDP, DMK, TMC, AGP, SP, KCP, MPVC, Cong-T) and four Left Front parties (CPI-M, CPI, FB, RSP). Deve Gowda's name was proposed by the CPI(M) leader Somnath Chatterjee and seconded by leaders of all thirteen parties constituting the United Front. By this time it was clear that the BJP government's fate was sealed. Vajpayee formally moved the confidence motion on 27 May and after debate on 28 May, he announced his resignation without facing a vote on the floor of the Lok Sabha. The President accepted his resignation and asked him to continue until alternative arrangements were made.

Then the President invited Deve Gowda, the consensus leader of the United Front, to form the next government and prove his majority on the floor of the House. Gowda was sworn in on 1 June, 1996 with 21 Ministers including 12 Cabinet Ministers. Another interesting development at this time was the hurried formation of a Federal Front within the United Front by regional parties — DMK, TMC, TDP and AGP — on 31 May, the eve of the swearing in of the UF government. A brainchild of Chandrababu Naidu, the Chief Minister of Andhra Pradesh, the Federal Front with 58 MPs was supposed to function as a pressure group within the United Front. With the aim of planning a common strategy and joint action on issues common to States *vis-à-vis* the Centre, the Federal Front was designed to be an instrument of regional parties to assert themselves at the Centre. The United Front drafted a Common Minimum Programme agreed upon by all partners as a guide to action for the new government.

The United Front won the confidence vote on 12 June, 1996 with the support of the Congress(I). Narasimha Rao, the Congress(I) president, affirmed that the Congress would not allow the government "fall under any circumstances".[27] Thus a genuine coalition government consisting of thirteen parties committed to a common action programme, and propped up by a larger party without participation, came to be established for the first time at the Centre.

Parties of the United Front

National Front			Left Front		
JD	–	45	CPI (M)	–	32
TDP	–	16	CPI	–	12
DMK	–	17	FB	–	3
TMC	–	20	RSP	–	5
SP	–	17			
AGP	-	5			
MPVC	–	2			
Kerala Cong.	–	1			
Cong. T	–	4	TOTAL	-	179

The Gowda Ministry could not complete one year, for Sitaram Kesri, the then Congress (I) President, handed over a letter to the President of India, Shanker Dayal Sharma on 30 March, 1997 conveying the decision of the Congress (I) to withdraw support "with immediate effect" and demanding the resignation of Deve Gowda.[28] Congress President accused the government of trying to marginalise the Congress and not taking serious efforts to check communal, divisive and separatist forces in the country. The Congress Working Committee supported Kesri's decision and authorised him to take appropriate action "for staking claim to form the government". But many Congress leaders themselves were surprised at the sudden move of the Congress President. Although a number of charges had been listed in the letter addressed to the President of India, the real reason lay elsewhere.[29] The Gowda government had by this time decided to reopen investigation in the Tanwar murder case in which Sitaram Kesri was allegedly involved. There were also official moves to launch FERA violation cases against fifteen Congress Working Committee members as well as to question Sonia Gandhi in the Bofors investigation case. In these circumstances the Congress felt the need of having a friendly Prime Minister at the Centre. Deve Gowda, it was felt, was not friendly to the Congress President in spite of his being dependent on the latter and had spared no means to hit him hard or belittle him. The CPI(M) General Secretary Harkishen Singh Surjeet was dead opposed to any change of leadership and insisted that the UF alone would decide who the Prime Minister should be. So Sitaram Kesri wanted to form the government himself as Premier and hoped that he could get the support of some non-Left constituents of the United Front in the effort. He wrote to the President claiming himself to be able to form a government although the Congress had only 142 members in the Parliament.

All the Left parties in the United Front unilaterally rejected the idea of supporting a Congress-led government or of joining a coalition with Kesri as its head. As the possibility of getting the United Front support eluded, the Congress came down to accepting any other person as the United Front Prime Minister. But, Deve Gowda decided not to step down and was ready for a trial of strength on the floor of the House. The United Front needed 70 MPs more to survive once the Congress decided to withdraw support. After twelve hours of debate on 11 April, 1997, Deve Gowda lost the confidence motion and was asked by the President to continue until alternative arrangements were made.

Uncertainty prevailed in the political scene for a week owing to the firm stand of the Janata Dal and the Left Front against any change of leadership. The Congress (I) made it clear that they were prepared to offer support to the United Front if Deve Gowda was removed. Leaders of the Federal Front were, on the other hand, willing to make a compromise with a view to avoiding a mid-term poll. So a new leader had to be chosen who was likely to be acceptable to all Front partners as well as to the Congress. There were a few persons willing to be considered unlike on the previous occasion. The CPI (M) General Secretary successfully blocked the chances of leaders whom they did not like to see as Prime Minister.[30] Laloo Prasad Yadav, the Bihar Chief Minister and the Janata Dal president, was blocked on the ground that he was facing corruption charges on a big scale. Mulayam Singh Yadav, the Samajwadi chief, was blocked because of recent embitterment between the SP and the CPI. G.K. Moopanar was disliked because of his friendly relations with Sonia Gandhi. The Marxists are reported to have apparently given two reasons for blocking him: (1) that the leader should come from the largest single party in the Front; (2) that the Prime Minister should come from the north Indian States this time to stall the progress of the BJP in the Hindi belt. In spite of Moopanar being the front runner, neither DMK nor TDP came forward to propose his name. In the last stage Deve Gowda suggested S.R. Bommai, another leader from Karnataka, as he did not want Moopanar to emerge as his successor. Gujral turned out to be the final choice and his candidature was endorsed by the Front's Steering Committee. The CPI (M) did not project any candidate of their own, but put forward their criteria for selecting the Prime Minister. They also decided to keep away from the Ministry. Decks were cleared finally when the Congress submitted another letter to the President on 18 April, 1997 saying that the party would support the United Front government if Deve Gowda was replaced by another leader of the alliance. So the gentlemanly and sophisticated politician and External Affairs Minister I.K. Gujral was elected as leader of the United Front on 19 April, 1997. Gujral was sworn in as Prime Minister on 21 April and he won the confidence vote in the Lok Sabha on 22 April.

The fate of the Gujral Ministry came to be tested within six months when the Jain Commission report was submitted. A Commission had been appointed by the Central Government on 23 August, 1991 under Justice Milap Chand Jain to inquire into the assassination of Rajiv Gandhi and find out if there was any conspiracy element behind it. The first report was submitted on 28 August, 1997 and placed on the Table of both Houses of Parliament on 20 November, 1997. The report pointed out that the LTTE was operating with the help of the DMK government and that the LTTE could not have killed Rajiv Gandhi without support and assistance from the DMK government and a section of DMK leaders.[31] The Congress President reacted immediately and asked the United Front government to drop the DMK Ministers. The Congress (I) was prepared for any talk with the Front only after the dismissal of the DMK Ministers.

In fact the Congress (I) was planning to overturn the Gujral Ministry by February next so as to avoid the presentation of a second budget by the United Front.[32] For they felt that a second budget would make the Congress weaker. The report had leaked out and the indictment of DMK was known before it was placed on the floor of the House. This was a heaven-sent opportunity for the Congress (I) who wanted to use it for creating a rift in the United Front, and they hoped to get the support of some constituents of the United Front.

Prime Minister Gujral rejected the demand of the Congress to dismiss the DMK Ministers and the whole United Front stood united on this issue. The Congress would have been contented with the "temporary removal" of the portfolio of Murasoli Maran, for it was a question of self-respect for the Congress not to support people who were allegedly involved in the murder of their leader.[33] But the DMK was strongly opposed to any compromise, and was encouraged to take a firm stand by the anti-Gujral lobby, in the UF led by the former Prime Minister Deve Gowda.

Meanwhile the Congress (I) again toyed with the idea of forming a government under their leadership, but none of the United Front partners was willing to join the Congress or tender support from outside. At last the Congress Working Committee decided on 28 November, 1997, to withdraw support to the Gujral Ministry with immediate effect. The decision was communicated to the President of India and on the same day, 28 November, 1997, the Gujral Ministry resigned. Although the majority of MPs belonging to all political parties were not inclined to face another election, there was no alternative. The President consulted constitutional experts and finally took the decision to dissolve the Lok Sabha and hold fresh elections. Gujral was asked to continue until alternative arrangements were made.

The First BJP-led Coalition, 1998

Coalition Formation

When the thirteen-day BJP government stepped out of office it had only three allies with it —the Samata party, the Shiv Sena and the Haryana Vikas party. Having failed to win over more members to keep itself in power, the BJP was convinced of the need to widen its net and win more allies to gain power. So in the 1998 elections it took the pragmatic approach of shelving the fundamentalist issues like the *Mandir*, Uniform Civil Code and Article 370, and thus made itself acceptable to other parties who had so far treated the BJP as unacceptable. They might have felt that the fundamentalist stance on Hindutva might not help them to expand beyond the Hindi belt. So the BJP strove to win over regional parties to get into new areas, particularly the south. It became imperative for the BJP to acknowledge the importance of the regional parties in their respective areas and align with them on their own terms. Although this was itself a matter of humiliation, the BJP could not dispense with it in the game of winning numbers. On the other hand, the regional parties with which the BJP decided to align this time were also at their loose ends, waiting for an opportunity to latch on to a national party to get into the Centre. AIADMK of Tamil Nadu and TDP (Parvathi) of Andhra Pradesh were under threat of extinction, having lost terribly in the preceding elections. Lok Shakti of Karnataka formed by Ramakrishna Hegde, Biju Janata Dal of Orissa led by Biju Patnaik and Trinamul Congress of West Bengal led by Mamata Banerjee were new in the arena and wanted to test their strength for the first time. The common interests brought the BJP and these regional parties together. Thus the BJP retained the relationship with the former allies — Samata, Akali Dal, Shiv Sena and Haryana Vikas party — and entered into new alliance with regional parties in Tamil Nadu, Orissa, Andhra Pradesh, Karnataka, West Bengal and Uttar Pradesh. The total came to sixteen and thus exceeded the constituents of the United Front.

BJP Alliance Statewise[34]

State		Alliance party/parties
Andhra Pradesh	:	Telugu Desam Party (Parvathi)
Bihar	:	Samata Party
Haryana	:	Haryana Vikas Party
Karnataka	:	Lok Shakti (R.K. Hegde)
Maharashtra	:	Shiv Sena
Orissa	:	Biju Janata Dal
Punjab	:	Akali Dal (Badal)
Tamil Nadu	:	AIDMK, MDMK, PMK, Tamil Nadu Rajiv Congress and Janata Party
Uttar Pradesh	:	Loktantrik Congress, Janatantrik BSP, Janata Dal (Rajaram)
West Bengal	:	Trinamul Congress

The United Front, on the other hand, consisting of thirteen parties while in power had lost its cohesion and failed to reach agreement on seat adjustment in UP, Bihar and Tamil Nadu. Further differences persisted among constituents particularly on economic issues despite the release of a Common Minimum Programme and Joint Policy Declaration. The Left parties prepared a separate manifesto emphasising the differences with the Minimum Programme of the UF.[35] Moreover the UF failed to project a common leader or Prime Ministerial candidate.

The Congress (I) had entered into State-level adjustments with a few parties — RJD, RPI, ML, KCM and RJP — although it had not acknowledged the arrangement as a national alliance. The Congress felt a little rejuvenated on account of the "Sonia factor", with Sonia Gandhi having agreed to campaign for the party.

Election Results, 1998

The final tally in the 1998 elections came out to be as follows:

BJP and allies	251
United Front	96
Congress and allies	166
Others	22
TOTAL	535

However, the sixteen constituents of the BJP-led alliance had been reduced to thirteen when the final results came. So the BJP had to accommodate only thirteen parties in the new government they had to form. The seats were as given below :

BJP	178
AIADMK	18
Samata	12
BJD	9
SAD	8
Trinamul	7
Shiv Sena	6
Lok Shakti	3
PMK	4
MDMK	3
TRC	1
JP	1
HVP	1
TOTAL	**251**

Cabinet Formation

Unlike the 11th Lok Sabha where the United Front and the Congress together had 330 members, the 12th Lok Sabha witnessed an equal balancing between the ruling and opposition parties. Having failed to reach a majority, the BJP-led alliance could form only a minority government, and as such the question of its durability was in doubt. But the prospects of forging an anti-BJP combine was even less daunting. So evidently the chances of a BJP led government were brighter this time.

However, coalition management was going to be beset with problems. The BJP had to accommodate some of the most temperamental personalities of Indian politics. "Besides old friends like the temperamental Shiv Sena chief Bal Thackerey and the volatile George Fernandes, the BJP will have to cope with the autocratic AIADMK supremo J. Jayalalitha and the fire-brand Trinamul Congress leader Mamata Banerjee, not to mention ... Subramanian Swamy who feels the Finance Minister's job is his rightful due".[36] Further as most of these new allies were in opposition in their respective States, their demands on the Centre threatened to multiply.

Such pulls and pressures had been in evidence no sooner than the election results were out. Jayalalitha who along with her four allies in Tamil Nadu commanded 27 MPs was giving the BJP sleepless nights even before Vajpayee was sworn in. She stunned the BJP as well as others by the announcement that she would extend only outside support to the Vajpayee government.[37] Then she made a retreat by saying that she was firm in her support to the BJP, but proved herself unreliable by the statement that she would take decisions in keeping with "the current situation". She was basically interested in overthrowing the DMK government in Tamil Nadu even if it involved unconstitutional means. Keeping such a person in good humour was perhaps the most demanding matter for the Prime Minister.

Equally problematic was the offer of "unconditional support" made by the Haryana Lok Dal Rashtriya (HLD-R) leader Om Prakash Chautala despite the BJP's alliance with Haryana Vikas Party. Nobody was prepared to believe that Chautala was concerned about political stability and every body felt sure that he would demand his pound of flesh. Other regional leaders also had their regional sensitivities and personal ambitions.

Parleys started even before the results were completely out. BJP began informal discussions with friendly parties in its bid to achieve the magic figure of 272 members in the Lok Sabha. The Congress and the United Front also were making separate attempts to explore the possibilities on their part. The United Front was most strongly committed to forming a non-BJP government in the event of a hung Parliament.[38] The Congress President Sitaram Kesri appeared hopeful and held discussions with Sonia and other Congress leaders about the prospects particularly in the context of BJP's failure in gathering enough support.[39] Meanwhile the TDP decided not to extend support to the Congress, but sit in the opposition and tender "issue-based" support to the BJP-led government.[40] The TDP decision gave further confidence to the BJP although the AIADMK had poured cold water by the announcement not to join the Ministry. TDP preferred to remain neutral in the Lok Sabha when a confidence motion would be voted upon. Chances for a non-BJP government were finally sealed when RSP and Forward Bloc of the Left parties announced their decision not to support the Congress.

Since the Congress and the United Front were not making claims to form the government, it was easy for the President K. R. Narayanan to take a decision. He asked Vajpayee, who had been formally elected leader of the BJP Parliamentary party by this time, whether he would be "able and willing" to from a stable government. Vajpayee promised to present documents to back his claim of support from 262 members out of 539 members at the time. However, he was able to present letters of support of 240 members only when he met the President on 12 March, 1998.[41] This was so because of the last minute game played by AIADMK leader Jayalalitha who refused to give a letter of support in spite of her earlier pronouncements. To the contrary, she was reiterating her demand for the dismissal of DMK government in Tamil Nadu. She had other personal demands too. She wanted the Finance portfolio to be given to Subramanian Swamy and other 'plum posts' for her other men although she denied herself to have made such demands. Accoring to reports, Jayalalitha had also hinted that the cases filed against her be withdrawn.[42]

The three-member MDMK, a partner of AIADMK in Tamil Nadu elections, who had intimated directly to the President of its support to BJP by fax now seemed to be retreating to remain with AIADMK. BJP had claimed the support of 228 of the pre-poll partners including MDMK and 12 outsiders, i.e. 4 of Haryana Lok Dal-R, 2 of Arunachal Congress, 1 of Sikkim Democratic Front and independents including Maneka Gandhi, Buta Singh, Satnam Singh Kainth and one MP each from Mizoram and Manipur. The total number 240 was thus 22 down from 262 claimed by the BJP two days earlier.[43] If MDMK was to remain with AIADMK the number would come down further by three. Vajpayee and Advani again talked to Jayalalitha over phone, but failed to persuade her to tender the letter of support. Since the prospects of a BJP government was getting dimmer, the President invited the Congress and United Front leaders and discussed the political situation. Rekindled with hopes, they sought time to explore the alternative possibility. However, informal contacts had continued between the BJP leaders and Jayalalitha, and on

14 March she tendered a letter of "total and unconditional" support to the BJP and the letter was submitted to the President.

At this time there was a sort of a coup in the Congress, and the Congress Working Committee decided to replace Sitaram Kesri by Sonia Gandhi as President. Sonia informed the President of India of her party's decision not to stake claim to form a government. This smoothened the way for the President who invited Vajpayee on 15 March, 1998 to form the government and prove majority support on the floor of the House within ten days. In the numbers game that was to follow, the BJP and allies were to constitute 264 members out of 539. TDP with 12 members were to remain neutral and all others in the opposition numbered 263. This was a precarious margin of one vote's lead, but it was a decisive advantage for the BJP.[44]

Further parleys between Vajpayee's emissary Jaswant Singh and Jayalalitha at the latter's residence at Chennai brought her round to agree to join the government. Thus the AIADMK, PMK and TRC were to join the Ministry although Jayalalitha's plea for including Subramanian Swamy was not accepted. BJP leadership also agreed to incorporate the six-point charter of demands brought up by Jayalalitha in the National Agenda.

Once it was clear that Vajpayee had to form the government, he started conferring with pre-poll allies about their nominees as Ministers and their preferences for portfolio.[45] There were already rumours about the names of important ministers and the allocation of important portfolios. It was generally accepted that Home would go to L.K. Advani, the BJP President and No. 2 man in government. Finance was a bone of contention; Vajpayee had his preference for Jaswant Singh who had been allotted the same portfolio in the 13-day Cabinet. Although he had been defeated this time, Vajpayee wanted to retain his services. But the BJP hard core did not like him. The party also preferred Murali Manohar Joshi to take the HRD Ministry. Allies had their own preferences, Jayalalitha having made them clear already. Akali Dal was interested in the Agriculture Ministry. An Akali MP who was also a member of the State Legislative Assembly refused to vacate his seat in the Assembly unless he got a Ministerial berth at the Centre.

Although the date of the Ministry's swearing in was fixed as 19 March, the list of Ministers and their portfolios could not be finalised even on 18 March. The last minute decision of George Fernandes to join the Ministry upset the pecking order carefully prepared by Vajpayee and Advani.[46] Thus Ministry making proved to be nightmarish to the BJP who had to balance the claims of the allies and those of the senior leaders within the party. Added to this was the request of Subramanian Swamy, who had been left out of the list, to Jayalalitha to permit him a "conscience vote" during the motion of confidence.[47]

Vajpayee took office on 19 March, 1998 along with a 42-member Council of Ministers, comprising 21 Cabinet rankers and 21 Ministers of State.[48] Of the 21 Cabinet members, 10 were from the BJP, 9 from among the pre-poll allies and 2 Independents — Ram Jethmalani and Buta Singh. Among the allies AIADMK and Samata got two Cabinet posts, and other allies — Akali Dal, Lok Shakti, Biju Janata Dal, Tamizhaka Rajiv Gandhi Congress and Shiv Sena — one Cabinet post each. Trinamul Congress did not join the Ministry and BJP's lone MP from West Bengal — Sikdar — could not be included owing to opposition from Mamata Banerjee. The notable absentee was Jaswant Singh who preferred to stay away owing to opposition from the 'swadeshi lobby' in the BJP. Among the 21 Ministers of State, there were 13 from BJP and 8 from the allies.

Immediately after the swearing in of the Council of Ministers came the question of the election of the Lok Sabha Speaker. The BJP was inclined to taking the Speakership for itself and giving the Deputy Speakership to the Congress. But when the BJP floated the idea of evolving a consensus on the issue, the Congress–UF combine projected P.A. Sangma for Speaker. Standing on the verge of a confidence vote, the BJP was willing to concede the post to the opposition, and Vajpayee almost congratulated Sangma personally about his prospects. Suddenly came the *volte face* on the part of TDP chief who hitherto had claimed to remain neutral on the Speaker's election.[49] Thus there were two candidates in the fray — P.A. Sangma of the Congress and G.M.C. Balayogi of TDP. BJP-led coalition was forced to accept Balayogi's candidature and elect him Speaker. After three days Vajpayee's confidence motion was put to vote and Vajpayee won by the positive vote of the TDP. The voting breakdown was as follows :[50]

Total strength including nominated	-	545
Elections to be held	-	4
Those who have not taken oath	-	2
Effective strength	-	539
Effective strength without Speaker	-	538
Ruling combine with TDP and 2 nominated	-	274
Congress and UF	-	261
Absent	-	1
Abstention (National Conference)	-	2

Coalition Management

Although the Ministry-making exercise was finished amicably, the Prime Minister's nerves were stretched time and again within a month.[51] First, it was the case of not including Jaswant Singh in the Cabinet under pressure of the RSS. Second, it was the question of giving independent charge of revenue and banking to R.K. Kumar, a confidante of Jayalalitha. Third, it was the demand of AIADMK to dismiss the DMK government in Tamil Nadu. When the Opposition raised the issue of DMK government's dismissal in the Parliament, Vajpayee had to make it clear that the dismissal of DMK government under Article 356 was not a priority for the government. But there was an equally strong demand from the Samata leaders for the application of Article 356 against the RJD government of Bihar.

Jayalalitha used to bring out personal enmities publicly and demand governmental action against persons whom she disliked. Once she demanded action against Sun TV which was owned by Murasoli Maran, a Cabinet Minister at the Centre and the nephew of DMK leader M. Karunanidhi. She had also demanded the resignation of three Cabinet Ministers — Ramakrishna Hegde, Ram Jethmalani and Buta Singh — with at least two of whom she had personal scores to settle.

Jayalalitha's obsession with DMK's ouster had led to raising the issue in a big way in the Lok Sabha and Rajya Sabha in June 1998. The immediate provocation for the same seems to be the order of a special court in Chennai to attach the properties of Jayalalitha and her confidante Sasikala Natarajan.[52]

Apart from the AIADMK there were other allies too who were unhappy about the situation. Resenting the big brother attitude of the BJP, some constituents led by the Samata party planned to form a pressure group within the coalition.[53] Leaders of Samata and Shiromani Akali Dal felt aggrieved that they were not being consulted on crucial issues like the Women's Reservation Bill and the creation of new States like Uttaranchal and Vananchal in which they had special interest. The Samata had demanded a sum of Rs. 50,000 crore for Bihar toward compensation if a separate Vananchal State was to be created.[54] Akalis threatened to withdraw support if Udham Singh Nagar was included in the proposed Uttaranchal State. AIADMK leader also welcomed the idea of a pressure group inside the coalition for her own reasons.[55] However, their efforts to rope in Biju Janata Dal and Haryana Vikas Party into the inner alliance did not succeed.

The general elections to the Legislative Assemblies of Delhi, Rajasthan, Madhya Pradesh and Mizoram scheduled to be held in the month of November 1998 occasioned a dispute over seat sharing between some of the coalition partners. Lok Shakti leader Ramakrishna Hegde wanted to put up candidates in the four States and had met the BJP President and other leaders in this connection. The response of the latter was rather cold and this left a bitter feeling with the Lok Shakti. Further the electoral debacle of the BJP in their traditionally strong areas in Madhya Pradesh, Rajasthan and Delhi invited criticism from the coalition partners themselves. AIADMK, the largest ally of the BJP, was the first to express a note of disgruntlement. According to Jayalalitha, the electoral defeat reflected a sense of popular anger and disenchantment with the BJP led government.[56] Trinamul Congress spokesman Ajit Panja spoke of the electoral verdict as a reprimand for BJP's consistent record of neglect of its partners' interests.[57]

The Trinamul leader Mamata Banerjee, although not so aggressive as Jayalalitha of AIADMK, spared no occasion to criticise the BJP-led government of which it was an ally. She resigned from the Central Co-ordination Council to highlight the issue of spiralling prices of essential commodities although she continued to render support to the government. She did it with the hope of redeeming the image lost in the State politics at the time.[58] Their decision to observe December 6 as a black day to commemorate the demolition of Babri Masjid was an instance. Mamata joined the nation-wide protests against the attacks on Christians in Gujarat and Orissa. She demanded the resignation of Home Minister L.K. Advani for his failure to prevent the ghastly murder of the Australian missionary and his son in Orissa. She demanded the dismissal of the BJP Ministry in Gujarat for the failure to protect the minorities and of the Shiv Sena-BJP Ministry in Maharashtra on the cricket issue.[59]

The decision of the Central Government to effect a cut in food subsidy and increase the price of urea added one more issue for the acrimonious criticism of the allies.[60] Chandrababu Naidu, the TDP chief, called for the immediate withdrawal of price hike on foodgrains supplied from ration shops. Om Prakash Chautala, the INLD leader of Haryana, threatened to withdraw support to the Vajpayee government on this issue. AIADMK also joined the critics of the price hike and demanded a roll back. There was a general discontentment against the way the decision was taken without taking the allies into confidence. "Arriving at major decisions without consulting coalition partners is not morally right", they held.[61]

Within a few days the threat of the INLD became a reality when Chautala announced withdrawal of support to the BJP government.[62] But the government continued to take decisions without consulting the allies. The next instance of such a decision was the hike on telecom rates, announced on 9 March, 1999. The new rates which were to come into force on 1 April, 1999 had to be held back on account of a threat from Trinamul Congress to boycott the Lok Sabha session in protest.

AIADMK chief's relationship with the Prime Minister was getting strained on several counts. She was putting forth demands on the Prime Minister and the latter failed to meet all of them. Her demand for the removal of the Enforcement Directorate Chief, M.K. Bezbaruah was conceded, but her demand for replacing him by her own nominee could not be met.[63] Her demand for the replacement of Revenue Secretary

N.K. Singh by the Banking Secretary, C.M.Vasudevan, was met half way. N.K. Singh was shifted to the Prime Minister's Office, but the post was filled by Javed Chaudhary. But her other major demands like dismissal of DMK government in Tamil Nadu, appointment of Subramanian Swamy as Finance Minister, etc. remained unfulfilled. She was becoming restive and more bitter day by day and went to the extent of indirectly accusing the Prime Minister of accepting bribes from a media baron who was being investigated into for alleged FERA violations.

No Prime Minister would bear such aggressive behaviour on the part of an ally. Vajpayee, as a countermove, wanted to drop the AIADMK ministers and even prevented Janardanan, AIADMK Minister, from proceeding on a foreign tour.[64] However, he was persuaded to hold his fire and wait to see Jayalalitha walking out.

The political scene in Tamil Nadu was changing. The MDMK leader "Vaiko" Gopalaswamy, an electoral ally of AIADMK, decided to extend unconditional support to the BJP government. And a few others of the AIADMK allies also showed willingness to join the government. DMK chief Karunanidhi, a strong pillar of the UF, added a new dimension by stating that his party would support "all good schemes of the BJP".[65] He also added that all elected governments should be allowed to govern for five years. This indicated the possibility of a new political alignment at the Centre as well as in Tamil Nadu. The rift within the AIADMK alliance became so deep that the Pattali Makkal Katchi leader Ramdoss warned the BJP government against yielding to Jayalalitha's pressures and against divesting Minister Vazhappady Ramamurthy of the petroleum portfolio.[66]

The election of the Speaker and of the Deputy Speaker of Lok Sabha also added to the discontent. BJP's official stance that the Speakership should go to the ruling coalition and Deputy Speakership to the Opposition could not go smoothly. As regards Speakership, the BJP had its own candidate, but the last minute thrust made by Chandrababu Naidu in imposing a TDP candidate, G.M.C. Balayogi, shattered the hopes of BJP. However, Jayalalitha alleged that the BJP had agreed on the election of Balayogi of TDP without consulting the coalition partners, and so when the election of the Deputy Speaker came up Jayalalitha supported the Congress candidate in order to avoid BJP's appropriating the post for itself.[67]

The proposed Cabinet expansion announced by the Prime Minister on 12 January, 1999 had to be put on hold on account of the stiff stance taken by the allies. The Prime Minister, it was reported, wanted to get half the posts for BJP and distribute the rest among the allies.[68] He entrusted George Fernandes with the task of contacting the allies and working out the arithmetic of representation. Jayalalitha seemed to have wanted to establish that she had the final authority to decide the representation from Tamil Nadu. She wanted four posts, besides stripping Ramamurthy of the Petroleum Portfolio. Mamata Banerjee, insisting on the Railway portfolio, evaded any contact from the Prime Minister's Office.[69] The Akali chief informed the Prime Minister that the Akali nominee, P. Chandumajara, was no longer interested in joining the Cabinet. Samata Party was aggressive about retaining the Railway portfolio and further wanted two of their important leaders — Digvijay Singh and Abdul Gaffoor — to be accommodated.[70]

Within the BJP it was not all going smooth. The pulls and pressures within the party forced Vajpayee to shelve his plans for Cabinet expansion. There was demand for accommodating Sushama Swaraj as well as Sahib Singh Varma.[71] Problems were so intense that Vajpayee had to hold a day-long meeting with Advani and Thakre, two days before the expansion was scheduled, to discuss the pros and cons of effecting a Cabinet reshuffle at that time.[72] That made clear that Vajpayee did not have a free hand in Cabinet making even in relation to his own party. It was at about this time that Madan Lal Khurana, the Central Minister for Tourism and Parliamentary Affairs, was forced to submit his resignation owing to the hostility of the Sangh Parivar groups within the BJP.[73] The turmoil resulting from Khurana's resignation reflected the growing conflict within the ruling party between a group of pragmatists who wanted to proceed with the job of governance and a group of ideologues who were uncompromising. It was widely held that Khurana's fall was manoeuvred by the RSS. Even when it was apparent that Sahib Singh Varma could not steer BJP to an electoral victory in Delhi the RSS had resisted efforts to unseat him. Staunchly opposed to him, the RSS was eager to neutralise the 'Punjab lobby' that stood by Khurana.[74] Khurana's return as Chief Minister of Delhi would make him too powerful for the Sangh Parivar to tolerate. Since Kushabhau Thakre assumed charge as Party President Khurana found himself at odds with the new dispensation.

The open fight had necessarily to be ended by an amicable settlement. So the leaders agreed to creating an institutional mechanism to ensure smooth party-government relationship as well as to avoid lapses in communication between them in future. The measures were to include[75]: (i) the establishment of a programme monitoring unit and redressal grievance cell involving the Prime Minister's office and the party; (ii) daily interaction between Prime Minister's office and party office to ensure a common media policy; (iii) Ministers to spare an hour each week for BJP workers and to appoint one party functionary in each Minister's office; (iv) holding daily meetings between Vajpayee and Advani, besides fortnightly meetings among Vajpayee, Advani, Thakre and Sudarshan, the Secretary of RSS; (v) ensuring that the different wings of the Sangh Parivar work broadly in tandem; (vi) projecting Vajpayee as a people's man; (vii) consultation with party and RSS on policy decisions and political appointments; and (viii) interaction between the party and its allies at the grassroots level. The agreement was supposed to provide for a mutual check; but it was easier said than done.

The Sangh Parivar was trying to strangle the government by its dogmatic approach. The Vishwa Hindu Parishad's *Dharma Sansad* at Ahmedabad during 5-7 February, 1999 reflected a revision on the fundamentalist question of constructing the Ram temple at Ayodhya.[76] One section seemed unhappy about jeopardising the stability of the Central government over an issue that lost the political potential. The other group insisted that temple construction should be pursued to its logical end, considering the fact that a good portion of the work had been already completed. The consensus appeared to be in favour of deferring re-construction for two years. Yet the dominant militant group in the VHP appealed to the BJP to hold on to the Hindutva agenda. The VHP also outlined a 40-point "Hindu" agenda, and announced plans to mobilise opinion and create a "Hindu vote bank" in order to free the BJP from its dependence on the allies.[77]

The party leadership minced no words in directing criticism against the government and its policies. The BJP president Kushabhau Thakre gave vent to his ire against the dilution of the *swadeshi* plank in the proposed Insurance Regulatory Authority Bill and pointed that the government was not committed to its ideology.[78] But he was only voicing the anger of the RSS General Secretary and other hard core men at the government's departure from ideology. However, ultimately Thakre had to come round and approve a Statement drafted by the Prime Minister's Office calling on all BJP members of Parliament to "fully back the IRA Bill when it is introduced and ensure its successful passage". The government, it was added, was the best judge of the need for such a bill.[79] The tension within the party made the Prime Minister fretful enough to describe the Indian democracy as "hollow" and party politics as "criminalised".[80]

Admiral Bhagwat's issue became another thorn on the Prime Minister's crown.[81] This gave a handle to the critics of the government to beat the Defence Minister and hit the Prime Minister. Jayalalitha demanded the resignation of the Defence Minister at the Coordination Committee meeting on 27 March, 1999, and referred to his mishandling of the issue as well as to the allegation that he was harbouring militants.[82] She also demanded that Admiral Bhagwat be taken back. But the Prime Minister ruled out any change in George Fernandes' position and rejected the demand for the reinstatement of Bhagwat as Naval Chief.[83]

Jayalalitha aggravated the situation by meeting Sonia Gandhi at a tea party arranged by Subramanian Swamy on 29 March. This was a part of the calculated move to undermine the BJP-led government with the help of the Congress. The presence of former Prime Ministers — Narasimha Rao, Deve Gowda and Chandrashekhar — at the tea party added political significance.[84] Immediately after, she put forth a three-point set of demands on the Bhagwat issue and declared that her party's continuance in the government would depend on the latter's response. The demand included the reinstatement of Bhagwat, the constitution of a Joint Political Committee to probe into his sacking as also the expulsion of Fernandes.[85] Although she said that she would give a reasonable time limit for the disposal of her demands by the Prime Minister, she indicated that she was willing to desert the BJP-led coalition and strike an alliance with the Congress. "If the government was a train", she said, "the AIADMK was the engine. BJP was only the driver. The AIADMK could push the driver out, and drive the train on its own. The train would go on even if some bogies dropped out. Even if all the bogies dropped out, the engine could go to the next railway station and attach itself to another train and move on."[86] However, the Cabinet rejected the demands of Jayalalitha, and that was enough to provoke her to withdraw her two Ministers —Thambi Durai and Janardhanan — from the government.[87] The Prime Minister forwarded the resignation letters to the President, reportedly after asking Jayalalitha once more about the same. As the next move, Jayalalitha decided to step out of the Co-ordination Committee and started open manoeuvres to oust the BJP-led government.

The prospects of an alternative government were not clear. The CPI, CPI (M) and DMK denounced any combine that would include the AIADMK. But Jayalalitha carried on hectic activity by contacting MPs of various parties including the Republican Party of India, Indian Union Muslim League, Kerala Congress(M), RJD and the National Conference. Laloo Prasad Yadav, the leader of RJD, announced with glee that the next Prime Minister would be elected within five minutes of the resignation of Vajpayee. But nobody could see any clear picture of the next Prime Minister, probably many had nurtured hopes about getting a chance. In this nebulous situation created by her own *faux pas*, Jayalalitha submitted to the President of India, on 14 April 1999, a letter withdrawing her party's support to the BJP-led government.[88]

The President advised the Prime Minister to seek a vote of confidence in the Lok Sabha. Although the President had not fixed any time limit, the Prime Minister decided to have the motion moved on 15 April. There were new political alignments. The DMK, the permanent rival of AIADMK in Tamil Nadu, declared support to Vajpayee. The INLD was won over to the BJP side. The Congress which was hitherto reluctant to provide leadership to the anti-government moves now came out in the open. The Left Front also worked hard to win some groups to the anti-BJP camp. Sonia could persuade the Tamil Manila Congress leader to remain with them, despite their anti-Jayalalitha stance. The five-member Bahujan Samaj Party was decisive. Their last minute jump to the opposition sealed the fate of the government. H.S. Surjeet, Secretary-General of the CPI (M), was in touch with Kanshi Ram, the BSP leader. An early morning telephone talk between Sonia Gandhi and Ms Mayavati made the difference.[89] Some individual MPs also had crossed the floor to join either side against the official stance of their party leadership. Saifudeen Soz of the National Conference and the Akali rebel Chandumajra had voted with the opposition against their party decision. Chaoba Singh of the Manipur State Congress crossed over and voted for the government. However, the BJP government lost the confidence motion by a margin of one vote – 269 in favour and 270 against.[90]

The Second BJP-led Coalition 1999

Having lost the confidence vote, the fate of the first BJP-led coalition Ministry was sealed. And the Ministry continued as care-taker until after the next general elections to the 13th Lok Sabha in September-October 1999. The electoral confrontation took place mainly between the BJP-led National Democratic Alliance on the one hand and the Congress (I) on the other, the third front failing to fructify as a united force. The NDA facing the 1999 elections was different in character from the BJP-led alliance of 1998 elections, with some of the allies replaced and the total strength rising to form a grand coalition of 24 parties. A pre-poll alliance electorally, the NDA lacked in the necessary cohesion and ideological and programmatic fusion or agreement that genuine coalitions were characterised to have. Some of the allies were conditionally aligned, like the Trinamul Congress, Telugu Desam and the Indian National Lok Dal, having their vital interests rooted in State politics.[91] The Biju Janata Dal and the Janata Dal(U) also had similarly strong regional interests underpinning their alliance with the BJP at the national level. The INLD, TDP and DMK were new entrants into the NDA, having left their earlier secular allies of the United Front under regional compulsions. With some of the State Governments facing Assembly elections — Andhra Pradesh, Karnataka, Nagaland, Meghalaya, Manipur and Mizoram —the national and State interests of the parties had to be co-ordinated.

The NDA's national agenda had to be mellowed down by sidelining core issues like the Ram Temple, the Uniform Civil Code and Article 370 in order to soften the non-saffron parties. Lok Shakti leader and Union Commerce Minister Ramakrishna Hegde threatened to walk out of the ruling coalition if the BJP revived its stand on these core issues. However some of the partners like the TDP and Trinamul Congress remained outside the NDA's election manifesto and launched their own manifestos.[92] Thus there were contradictions within the NDA at the national level as well as at the State level. The NDA remained a loose and amorphous organisation without any clear control mechanism or norms of admission to membership. The Janata Dal (U) was admitted to the NDA on account of pressures exerted by Samata and Lok Shakti leaders in spite of objections raised by senior BJP leaders in Karnataka and Bihar. Further BJP did not consult the other partners of NDA when they decided to push out Haryana Vikas Congress and take in the INLD in its place.

The Congress (I) remained adamantly opposed to the idea of leading a coalition government at the Centre, and therefore there was no Congress-led alliance as such at the national level. There were a few electoral allies at the State level like the AIADMK in Tamil Nadu, RJD in Bihar and the traditional allies like the Muslim League and the Kerala Congress (M) in Kerala. Other anti-BJP parties like the Samajwadi Party and the BSP were equally anti-Congress (I) and were not inclined to have any electoral adjustment with either.

The election results cut down the representation of NDA's pre-poll partners in the Lok Sabha into fifteen, four of them having only one member each. The final election tally was as follows :

Election Results, 1999

Total Seats – 543

BJP & allies		Cong. (I) & allies		Left Parties		Other Parties	
BJP	182	Cong. (I)	114	CPI	4	BSP	14
BJD	10	AIADMK	10	CPI (M)	33	SP	26
DMK	12	KC (M)	1	FB	2	NC	4
HVC	1	ML	2	KC (J)	1		
INLD	5	RJD	7	RSP	3	Ind. & Others	21
JD (U)	21	RLD	2	Total	43	Total	65
Loktantrik	2	Total	136				
MDMK	4						
MGRADMK	1						
MSCP	1						
PMK	5						
SAD	2						
SS	15						
Trinamul	8						
TDP	29						
Ind.(Maneka)	1						
Total	299						

So the growth in BJP's strength in the Lok Sabha was marginal, having risen from 178 to 182, but the NDA's total strength was proportionately larger with a rise from 251 to 299. The National Conference, although not an ally of BJP in the elections, expressed willingness to join the NDA Ministry. But TDP which had seat adjustments with the BJP in Andhra Pradesh appeared to be deliberately non-committed about joining government, preferring to continue the policy of conditional and issue-based external support.[93] The situation manifested greater power for the regional parties within the coalition, the DMK, TDP, Trinamul and JD(U) being able to be more assertive than the non-BJP groups of the previous regime. There were indications that Mamata Banerjee was preparing for hard bargaining in order to bag at least three major portfolios like the Railways and the Home and to put Ajit Panja, her party man and former Congress minister at the Centre, in the new Cabinet. The Sikkim Democratic Front and the Mizo National Front with one member each also joined the BJP coalition. Thus the BJP's coalition partners increased in number from 13 in the previous Lok Sabha to 18 in the present one, including Maneka Gandhi.

The President of India had no difficulty in identifying the party and the leader to form the new Ministry unlike on earlier occasions, and as such he summoned Vajpayee to hand the letter of appointment.[94] Vajpayee went about the task of Ministry formation confidently, consulting the leaders of allied parties and then entrusting Jaswant Singh to do the follow up. George Fernandes was given the responsibility of sorting out individual ambitions within the JD(U). Vajpayee was under pressure from his party headquarters to ensure that there was party representation from each State, including States that had not returned a single BJP member. The TDP stayed out and was contented with the continuance of the existing Speaker, G.M.C. Balayogi, a TDP member. The list of Ministers was discussed and approved by senior colleagues like Advani, Jaswant Singh and Kushabhau Thakre.[95] Vajpayee who initially planned to have a 50-member Ministry was compelled to increase the number to accommodate claims of regions, coalition partners, experience, caste and other considerations.

The third Ministry led by A.B. Vajpayee was sworn in on 13 October 1999. It consisted of 25 Cabinet Ministers, 7 Ministers of State with independent charge and 37 other Ministers of State, in addition to the Prime Minister, totalling seventy.[96] The BJP was in a stronger position in the Ministry, having secured 47 Ministers out of 70, than in the previous Ministry which had a 50:50 proportion.[97] However there were disgruntled leaders in the alliance like Ramakrishna Hegde, Sikander Bakht and Sushama Swaraj who could not be included.[98] Some groups that joined the Ministry were not happy about the portfolios allotted to them.[99] Four of the 17 JD(U) Lok Sabha members from Bihar — Ram Vilas Paswan, Fernades, Nitish Kumar and Sharad Yadav — were given Cabinet berths and another member, Digvijay Singh, was made a Minister of State. Yet there were unhappy MPs in the JD(U).[100] Bihar had the highest representation in the Ministry as a State, yet of no advantage to the BJP politically. Tamil Nadu was represented by eight ministers, three of whom were of Cabinet rank, two Ministers of State with independent charge and three Ministers of State. Still dissatisfaction lingered over the allotment of portfolios.[101] Inside the BJP camp, the RSS was keen that the Defence portfolio should go to a BJP leader, preferably Advani. But Vajpayee kept it for George Fernandes probably thinking that a transfer of Defence portfolio at this time, in the backdrop of India's victory in the Kargil war, would be interpreted differently. Both DMK and TDP liked to have Finance for their men, but Yaswant Sinha was the favoured choice supported by the business interests as well as by the RSS. As regards the Speakership of Lok Sabha, the coalition and the Opposition unanimously decided to give it once again to G.M.C. Balayogi, the sitting Speaker of the 12th Lok Sabha and an MP of the TDP. The Deputy Speakership was given to P.M. Sayeed, the sitting Deputy Speaker and member of the Congress (I) under pressure of allies, particularly of the Trinamul Congress although the BJP had cherished hopes about getting the post for itself.[102]

The first year of governance passed without much turbulence, although not without occasional turmoils. Differences of opinion had cropped up between the coalition partners on national issues like increase in the price of petroleum products[103], revival of Ayodhya issue by the Sangh Parivar[104] and attack on Christian missionaries by the militant communal elements. A statement made by Vajpayee that the demand for the construction of a temple at Ayodhya was an expression of national sentiments was vehemently criticized by the coalition partners like DMK, TDP and Trinamul as well as by the Opposition parties. It was even doubted that Vajpayee was favourable to the "hidden agenda" of the BJP and of the Sangh Parivar, and was appealing to the Hindu voters of UP in the context of the forthcoming elections of April 2001.[105] The regional parties in the coalition, particularly the Trinamul Congress, DMK and TDP had always been constrained by their State-based interests and their political vision shortened by the State Assembly elections. Mamata's histrionics played in the wake of a hike in petrol and LPG prices and her threatened withdrawal from the Cabinet on the basis of this issue were meant to humour the electorate of West Bengal.[106] Her continued demand for the dismissal of the Marxist-led government of West Bengal, in spite of the Centre's rejection of the proposition to apply Article 356 in West Bengal, was a part of the poll-oriented political tactics.[107] Despite this kind of political games played by the coalition partners to strengthen their bargaining positions within the Ministry and by the Sangh Parivar to tighten its hold inch by inch into the BJP power, there seems to have developed a consensus among them to pull on together. The exit of *Pattali Makkal Katchi* from the coalition and the resignation of its two Ministers in February 2001 were occasioned by regional considerations alone, as the party thought it advisable to latch on to the AIADMK in the State Assembly elections of April-May 2001.[108] The PMK had no disagreement with the BJP; nor was its exit from the BJP camp meant to shaken the Ministry. But the PMK preferred to shift its alliance to the AIADMK camp on more pragmatic considerations of favourable payoffs in the State Assembly elections than of any ideological or emotional reasons.

Co-ordination Council at the Centre

The concept of a Co-ordination Council to ensure the smooth co-operation of coalition allies was accepted rather late at the Centre. The United Front governments under Deve Gowda and I.K. Gujral failed to institute a common forum for the coalition. There was a steering committee exclusively for the UF partners and the proposal for a Co-ordination Council including the Congress did not materialise. The Congress President was not willing to be controlled by a co-ordinating body as he was eager to have an opportunity to withdraw support.

While Gujral was elected Parliamentary leader of the UF, his appointment as Prime Minister was not all smooth. The President insisted on the creation of a formal arrangement for co-ordination with the supporting party. In fact Gujral was invited to form the government only after he agreed, in a joint letter with the Congress President Sitaram Kesri, to set up a mechanism of co-ordination consisting of five members each from the Congress and the UF.[109] However, the credit for installing such a council went to the BJP government. Some partners like the Trinamul Congress had initially proposed the creation of a Co-ordination Committee, but its creation was delayed owing to lack of interest on the part of some other partners. It was widely known that the AIADMK leader Jayalalitha had preferred to be free of any such control mechanism.

The Co-ordination Council was however set up by the Prime Minister on 21 April, 1998 to manage his temperamental 18-party allies.[110] It was to consist of five representatives of the BJP including the Chairman, and thirteen representatives of the other partners.[111] There was to be no rigidity regarding membership, as more representatives could be specially invited to attend meetings. Initially only the electoral allies were included, and the Premier was given power to decide if post-election allies were to be included. Vajpayee, the Prime Minister, was to be the Chairman and Jaswant Singh was made convener. Although the creation of the Co-ordination Council had been decided by the BJP and the allies in early March 1998, the matter was not given priority.[112] The first meeting of the Council was held on 9 May 1998 and it came off "successfully" in the thick of bargaining without sensitive issues being raised or thrashed out.[113] At least some quarters started thinking about strengthening the co-ordination process by holding frequent meetings of the forum and deliberating on major issues before policy announcements were made.[114] Suggestions like making the participation of constituents mandatory and ensuring the presence of a deputy to represent the group in the absence of the leader also came up.

Needless to say that no sincere efforts were made by the constituents including the BJP to make the Co-ordination Council an effective body. The BJP leaders often talked about "coalition *dharma*", but refused to practise what they preached.[115] The allies complained that they were not being consulted on major issues and that the Co-ordination Council meetings were held only to get decisions rubber-stamped.

Trinamul Congress which did not join the Ministry was unwilling to join the Co-ordination Council also initially. Although they joined the Council later on they spared no chance to criticise the government and in protest against some of the policies they withdrew membership of the body. AIADMK leader Jayalalitha also withdrew membership before resigning from the Cabinet.

Thus the Co-ordination Council could not be made use of as a forum for effective co-ordination of allies during the first

BJP-led coalition government. It became an object of contempt for the coalition partners, some of whom had not even liked to remain its members. Its status could not be improved during the second coalition too.

Personality Factor

There were three Prime Ministers in two years (1996-98); each one was unique in his own way. Deve Gowda was chosen as the Prime Ministerial candidate through a process of elimination, and being comparatively unknown outside Karnataka he was a dark horse that emerged on the national scene. Coming from a middle class agricultural background, he had risen to the Chief Ministership of Karnataka under the banner of the Janata Dal, the largest party in the United Front. With no command of Hindi and with a little of English, he tried to manage a vast country and an alliance of thirteen parties. Although dependent on the Congress support for his position, he showed scant respect for the Congress President Sitaram Kesri and often he tried to ignore him. It was his style of dealing with the Congress President and his violation of Congress' interests that led to the withdrawal of Congress support and to his own ignominious exit.

I.K. Gujral, generally described as a suave and refined gentlemanly politician, was neither hostile to the Congress nor authoritarian with the partners. But the ambitious Congress President, in his anxiety to protect the image of his party in the context of the Jain Commission report, wanted to try his chances once more. Both United Front Prime Ministers were dependent on outside support and had difficulty in managing the Congress more than the coalition partners.

Vajpayee was in a more strange company than the UF Prime Ministers were. Some of the allies who wanted to show themselves as superior to the Prime Minister brought in 'ego problems'. Some had ulterior motives in joining or supporting the government and sometimes made open efforts to promote them. The hard core of his own party were never indulgent towards his policy of compromise. The task of knitting these divergent strands into a cohesive unit and providing a semblance of collective responsibility demanded a herculean effort. Gupta and Bhaumik seemed to predict: "An easy going leader, Vajpayee is not known for either cunning or ruthlessness. He is most comfortable in mass politics, but the problems of coalitions are not resolved through thundering speeches. Nor is the party of much help. Most BJP leaders are inward looking and used to RSS inspired orderliness. They are usually at sea in dealing with people from a different political milieu. For governing with a wafer-thin majority, Vajpayee will need all the wily ingenuity of Bhairon Singh Sekhawat."[116] Wily though he is not, he has had to use political gimmicks like one-day fasting to sideline his opponents and win public sympathy.

He could accept a high degree of self-effacement to keep the coalition working. Being moderate in views and tolerant to minority groups, he was the one BJP leader most acceptable to the allies. But the personal ambition and the private manoeuvres of allies like J. Jayalalitha, Mamata Banerjee and Chandrababu Naidu kept him on tenterhooks all the time. Coalition experiments at the Centre thus proved that the personality of leaders was an important factor contributing to the maintenance of coalitions.

NOTES

1. R. Rajeevan, *The Role of National Opposition in India: 1984-89* (Ph.D. Thesis submitted to the University of Kerala, 1997), p. 108.
2. *Indian Express* (New Delhi), 17 May 1979.
3. Arun Gandhi, *Morarji Papers* (New Delhi, 1983), p. 226.
4. *Indian Express* (New Delhi), 16 July 1979.
5. R. Rajeevan, n.(1), p. 113.
6. *Hindustan Times* (New Delhi), 28 October 1987.
7. *Hindustan Times* (New Delhi), 29 Nov. 1987.
8. *Free Press Journal* (Bombay), 11 Jan. 1988.
9. R. Rajeevan, n.(1), pp. 164-65.
10. *Hindustan Times* (New Delhi), 12 October 1988.
11. R. Rajeevan, n.(1), p. 173.
12. *Indian Express* (New Delhi), 10 June 1989.
13. *Statesman* (New Delhi), 23 October 1989.
14. Amalendu Das Gupta, "Reversal of Roles, Opposition Loses Initiative", *Statesman* (New Delhi), 20 May 1989.
15. *The Hindu* (Madras), 29 November 1989.
16. *The Telegraph* (Calcutta), 29 November 1989.
17. *The Times of India* (New Delhi), 30 November 1989.
18. *Indian Express* (New Delhi), 2 December 1989.
19. *The Hindu* (Madras), 2 December 1989.
20. *The Hindu* (Thiruvanathapuram), 9 October 1999.

21. Meenu Roy, *Elections 1998*, NPH (Jaipur, 1999), p. 1.
22. *The Statesman* (New Delhi), 18 February 1996.
23. *Diary of Political Events,* Vol. 23, January–December 1996, Lok Sabha Secretariat, New Delhi.
24. Subhash C. Kashyap (ed), *Coalition Government and Politics in India* (New Delhi, 1997), p. 70.
25. *Diary of Political Events,* n. (23).
26. *Ibid.*
27. *Ibid.*
28. Meenu Roy, n.(21), p. 4.
29. *Ibid.*, p. 5.
30. *Politics India,* Vol.1, No. 12, June 1997, p. 44.
31. Meenu Roy, n. (21), p.8.
32. *Politics India,* Vol. II, No. 4, October 1997, p. 46.
33. Meenu Roy, n. (21), p. 9.
34. *Ibid.*, p. 179.
35. *The Hindu* (Thiruvananthapuram), 2 February 1998.
36. Swapan Das Gupta and Saba Naqui Bhaumik, "Crown of Thorns", *India Today,* 16 March 1998, p. 14.
37. *Ibid.*, p.15.
38. *The Hindu* (Thiruvananthapuram), 2 March 1998.
39. *The Hindu* (Thiruvananthapuram), 4 March 1998.
40. *The Hindu* (Thiruvananthapuram), 5 March 1998.
41. *The Hindu* (Thiruvananthapuram), 13 March 1998.
42. *Ibid.*
43. *Ibid.*
44. *The Hindu* (Thiruvananthapuram), 16 March 1998.
45. *The Hindu*, 17 March 1998.
46. *The Hindu*, 19 March 1998.
47. *Ibid.*
48. *The Hindu,* 20 March 1998.
49. *The Hindu* (Thiruvananthapuram), 22 March 1998.
50. *The Hindu* (Thiruvananthapuram), 25 March 1998.
51. *The Hindu* (Thiruvananthapuram), 20 April 1998.
52. *Telegraph,* 6 June 1998.
53. *The Pioneer*, 16 July 1998.
54. Suman K. Jha, "Sordid Politics of Coalition", *The Pioneer*, 21 August 1998.
55. *The Pioneer,* 16 July 1998.
56. Sukumar Muraleedharan, "A Debacle in Nine Months", *Frontline*, 18 December 1998, p. 5.
57. *Ibid.*
58. *The Hindu* (Thiruvananthapuram), 4 November 1998.
59. Bal Thackeray, the Shiva Sena Chief, had announced that he would block the Pakistani cricket team visiting India. This had raised a furore all over the country.
60. *The Hindu* (Thiruvananthapuram), 30 June 1999.
61. *The Hindu* (Thiruvananthapuram), 2 February 1999.

62. *The Hindu* (Thiruvananthapuram), 17 February 1999.
63. "Life After . . . ." *India Today,* 31 August 1998, pp. 19-20.
64. *Ibid.*
65. *Ibid.*
66. *Indian Express* (Kochi), 13 October 1998.
67. *The Hindu* (Thiruvananthapuram), 10 December 1998.
68. *The Hindu* (Thiruvananthapuram), 3 January 1999.
69. It may be remembered that the Trinamul Congress led by Mamata Banerjee had not so far joined the government.
70. *The Hindu* (Thiruvananthapuram), 14 January 1999.
71. Earlier Sushma Swaraj was a Cabinet Minister at the Centre and Sahib Singh Varma the Chief Minister of Delhi. When the Delhi Assembly election came BJP high command removed Varma from the Chief Ministership and put Sushma there, thinking that she would be able to recover the image of the party. But the party lost majority and Sushma also lost the election. Thus both Sushma and Varma waited to be placed in the Central Cabinet.
72. *The Hindu* (Thiruvananthapuram), 24 January 1999.
73. *The Hindu*, 31 January 1999.
74. V.Venkatesan, "The War Within", *Frontline,* 26 February1999, p.17.
75. Prabhu Chawla, "Ready to Battle", *India Today,* 21 December 1998, p. 22.
76. Sukumar Muraleedharan, "Disintegrating Coalition", *Frontline,* 26 February1999, p.8.
77. V. Venkatesan, n. (75), p. 20.
78. Prabhu Chawla, n. (76), p. 20.
79. *Ibid.*
80. Praful Bidwai, "Hindutva and moth-eaten governance ", *Frontline,* 26 February 1999, p. 16.
81. Admiral Vishnu Bhagwat was Chief of Naval Staff when he was dismissed by the BJP government on alleged security reasons. The dismissal became controversial as it provoked criticism among the service staff as well as politicians. Bhagwat sought to move the court against the dismissal. However the government stood firm in the decision and did not reinstate Bhagwat.
82. *The Hindu* (Thiruvananthapuram), 28 March 1999.
83. *The Hindu* (Thiruvananthapuram), 30 March 1999.
84. *The Hindu* (Thiruvananthapuram), 30 March 1999.
85. *The Hindu* (Thiruvananthapuram), 4 April 1999.
86. *Ibid.*
87. *The Hindu* (Thiruvananthapuram), 6 April 1999.
88. *Hindustan Times,* 15 April 1999.
89. *Hindustan Times,* 18 April 1999.
90. *Ibid.*
91. Sukumar Muraleedharan, "The Unaligned Players", *Frontline*, 24 September 1999, p.10.
92. V. Venkatesan, "Coalition Constraints", *Frontline*, 24 September 1999, p. 20.
93. *The Hindu* (Thiruvananthapuram), 8 October 1999.
94. *The Hindu* (Thiruvananthapuram), 12 October 1999.

95. *The Hindu* (Thiruvananthapuram), 13 October, 1999.
96. *The Hindu* (Thiruvananthapuram), 14 October, 1999.
97. V. Venkatesan "a Balancing Act", *Frontline,* 19 November 1999, p. 24.
98. Ramakrishna Hegde's inclusion was opposed by the BJP unit of Karnataka which had not taken kindly to Hegde's role in pushing the JD(U) into the NDA. Hegde's strategy was blamed as the cause for the miserable failure of NDA and the JD(U) in the elections to the Karnataka Assembly as well as to the Lok Sabha. This was consequent of the split of Janata Dal into JD(United) and JD (Secular) when a group led by Sharad Yadav, President of JD decided to merge with Lok Shakti and Samata Party. However the merger of the three groups did not materialize although the split of the JD remained so.

    Sikander Bakht, the only Muslim Minister in the previous Ministry, was dropped. Barnala was expected to represent Akali Dal in the new Ministry, but he could not win the elections. The other Akali MP, Sukhdev Singh Dhindse, refused to join the Ministry on account of opposition from Barnala. But he was sworn in next month.

    Sushma Swaraj, formerly a Union Minister and Delhi Chief Minister lost in the election against Sonia Gandhi in Bellary. A protégé of L.K. Advani, she had been promised a membership of Rajya Sabha and a place in the Ministry if she could not make out in the fight against Sonia Gandhi. She was not included in the first stage of Cabinet formation.
99. Shiv Sena leader Bal Thackeray expressed the view that their portfolios were not adequate. *The Hindu* (Kochi), 15 October 1999.
100. V. Venkatesan, "A Balancing Act", *Frontline*, 19 November 1999, p. 24.
101. V. Venkatesan, "A Cautious Approach", *Frontline,* 19 November 1999, p. 26.
102. *Ibid.*, p.27.
103. Diesel price was raised by about 40 per cent in October 1999 on the eve of the counting of votes to the Lok Sabha. This precipitated a countrywide strike by Lorry Owners' Association, but the government stood firm. TDP and JD(U) warned against any rise in prices of kerosene and LPG.
104. For a discussion of the developments relating to the Ayodhya Issue see *Frontline*, 7 January 2000, pp. 4-11.
105. Saba Naqvi Bhaumik "The Epic of Doublespeak", *Outlook*, 15 January 2001, pp. 30-32.
106. *Times of India*, 20 November 2000.
107. Saba Naqvi Bhaumik and Ashis K. Biswas, "The Bone Collector", *Outlook*, 22 January 2001, pp. 22-24.
108. *The Hindu* (Kochi), 6 February 2001.
109. *The Hindu* (Thiruvananthapuram), 9 October 1999.
110. *Indian Express* (New Delhi), 22 April 1998.
111. *Indian Express* (Kochi), 10 May 1998; *The Deepika* (Malayalam), 9 May 1998.
112. *The Hindu* (Thiruvananthapuram), 7 March 1998.
113. *M.P. Chronicle* (Bhopal), 11 May 1998.
114. *Times of India* (New Delhi), 9 July 1998.
115. Neena Vyas, "Physician, Heal thyself", *The Hindu*, 4 April 1999, p. 11.
116. "Crown of Thorns", *India Today,* 16 March 1998, p. 16.

4

COALITION POLITICS IN KERALA

Kerala has had the longest tradition of coalition politics in the country, having its roots in the Travancore-Cochin State even before the formation of the State of Kerala in 1956. Coalition politics in the State passed through several stages of experimentation and finally, settled for a polarised system which provides for alternative governments. This chapter analyses the history of coalition governments in Kerala and the ways of managing the same.

Coalition politics in Kerala can be traced to the 1952-53 Ministry of the erstwhile Travancore-Cochin State, a Part B State formed by the merger of the native kingdoms of Travancore and Cochin when India became independent. In the first general elections held in December-January 1951-52 no single party could secure majority of seats in the Travancore-Cochin Legislative Assembly. The Congress party, having secured 44 seats out of 108, formed a coalition government with the help of the Travancore Tamil Nadu Congress having 10 members, the Socialist party with 2 members and one nominated member. The Ministry could not last long due to differences between the Congress and the Tamil Nadu Congress regarding the Tamil speaking areas of Travancore. The withdrawal of support by the Tamil Nadu Congress led to the fall of the Ministry on 23 September 1953. The Assembly was dissolved and the Ministry continued as caretaker.

In the mid-term elections held in February 1954, the Congress got only 45 out of 118 seats. In a bid to avoid a possible Communist-led coalition government, the Congress extended outside support to the Praja Socialist Party which had only 19 members. Following a no-confidence motion the PSP Ministry fell and the Congress formed another coalition government with the support of 12 Tamil Nadu Congress members, 2 PSP defectors and one nominated member. This Ministry led by Panampilly Govinda Menon fell after thirteen months when six Congress legislators revolted against the Chief Minister in March 1956.

This was the situation in the Travancore-Cochin State when it was merged with the Malabar region of the Madras State to form the Kerala State under the States Reorganisation Act of 1956. General elections were held in February-March 1957 and the Communist Party secured a majority with 65 seats out of 126 including 5 Independents. The first Communist Ministry thus came to power in Kerala in April 1957 and ruled the State for 28 months at the end of which it was ousted by a mass upsurge that came to be designated *Vimochana Samaram.* In the elections that followed in 1960, the Congress-PSP-Muslim League alliance fought against the Communists and won 94 seats. A coalition Ministry was formed under Pattom A. Thanu Pillai of PSP as Chief Minister, with eight Congressmen and two other PSP members as Ministers. The Indian Union Muslim League had to be contented with the Speakership. The rivalry between the Chief Minister on one hand and the Congress Ministers R. Sankar and P.T. Chacko on the other led to the removal of Pattom from the State politics by his appointment as the Governor of Punjab. It was alleged that it was Pattom's authoritarianism, high handedness and rigidity that had led to the downfall of the coalition Ministry.[1] The Congress then formed a government of its own under the Chief Ministership of R. Sankar. Internal feuds of the Congress led to the fall of the Ministry in September 1964. The next elections held in March 1965 turned out to be infructuous as no government could be formed.

The elections of 1967 led to the victory of a seven-party alliance (*Saptamunnani)* led by the CPI(M) and to the formation of a coalition Ministry under E.M. Sankaran Namboodiripad as Chief Minister. Although this coalition had a comfortable majority with a strength of 117 members out of 133, internal dissensions and mismanagement brought about its fall in 1969. It was replaced by another coalition Ministry — the *Saptamunnani* minus the CPI (M) called the mini-front — headed by the CPI leader C. Achutha Menon. A split in the Indian

Socialist party, a constituent of the coalition, made the government shaky. The Legislative Assembly was dissolved on the advice of the Chief Minister and fresh elections held in September1970. The Congress and the mini-front together won this election and the second Ministry consisting of the CPI, RSP, IUML and PSP and headed by Achutha Menon was installed on 4 October, 1970. The Congress extended outside support in the beginning and joined the Ministry later. This was the first Ministry in Kerala to complete the full term, and its tenure was extended on account of the 'emergency' prevailing in the country at that time.

The next elections were held on 19 March, 1977, and United Front — the alliance of the Congress and the mini-front parties — became victorious. However, Kerala had to witness the fall of four ministries during the next three years owing to feuds within the Congress and jealousies between the coalition partners. In the next mid-term elections of January 1980 the Left Front led by the CPI(M) won majority and E.K. Nayanar formed the government. This government lasted for a few months only and Nayanar had to resign owing to withdrawal of support by some of the partners. The Assembly was held under suspension. There was a realignment of parties and the Congress (I) formed the next government under K. Karunakaran as Chief Minister. It had only a slender majority of one and had to resign when one member shifted loyalty. The next general elections were held on 10 March, 1982 in which two alliances fought each other — the United Democratic Front and the Left Democratic Front. The UDF got majority and K. Karunakaran formed the Ministry. It was the second Ministry in Kerala to complete the term.

There were three more elections — 1987, 1991 and 1996 — in which the LDF and the UDF fought against each other and formed governments by turn. The alliances remained stable throughout and the coalition governments completed their terms except for a change of Chief Ministership during the UDF regime of 1991-96.

The elections from 1970 to 1982 had shown unprincipled alliances between parties and factions which were ideologically poles apart. And the leading partners were in a mood to accept any one that came their way with a view to gaining strength.

This gave opportunity to the parties to bargain with the coalition leaders to gain the maximum payoff. Psychologically, it could be argued, they were searching for an identity and stable political relationship.

One unique feature of the Assembly election of 1987 was that the LDF had not included any communal group among its allies. The Marxists made proud claims regarding their secular character and antagonism to communal groups. But this policy was not adhered to in the succeeding elections, for they had to accommodate Kerala Congress(J) into their fold. However, in the elections of 1991 and 1996, the LDF and UDF partners were almost the same. This brought a stage of stable partnership among the two alliances in spite of splintering in the Kerala Congress and the Indian Union Muslim League.

This development signifies a bipolarisation of political parties — a two-party system within a multi-party system — in the State. An examination of the political programmes and the class character of the political parties in the two fronts will show that the polarisation achieved is not ideological, it is only political. Both UDF and LDF today include secular and communal parties in the usual sense of the term used.

From an ideological point of view CPI (M) and CPI may be considered proletarian in outlook, but Kerala Congress(J) and Janata Dal are not. Kerala Congress(J) represents the interests of upper class farmers in the State. Similar is the story about the UDF. The Congress is basically unhappy about its alignment with the Muslim League and the Kerala Congress, but the politics of survival force it to do so. A study made about the socio-economic background of the members of the 8th Kerala Legislative Assembly showed that the socio-economic back-grounds of the majority of Congressmen and the Marxists were substantially similar. Their political career was determined by their political background and training, and not by the economic and sociological factors.[2] The present political alliances have got stabilised by means of cohabitation and electoral adjustments.

Coalitions since 1960

Year of election	Partners led by Congress	Partners led by Communists/Marxists	Total number of seats
1960	Three party alliance of Congress (63), IUML (11), PSP (20)	No coalition. CPI (29), RSP (1), Independents (2)	126
1965	No coalition. Cong (36), KC (23), Swatantra (1). Independents (11)	Three party alliance. CPI (M) (40), SSP (13), IUML (6); CPI (3) separate	133
1967	No coalition. Cong (9), KC (5), Independents (6)	Saptamunnani. CPI (M) (52), CPI (19), IUML (14), RSP (6), SSP (19), KSP (1), KTP (2)	133
1970	Ruling Front: Cong (30), CPI (16), IUML (11), RSP (6), PSP (3) Independents (5)	Opposition Front: CPI (M) (30), SSP (6), ISP (3). Third Front: KC (12), Cong (0) (nil), Independents (11)	133
1977	Ruling Front: Cong (38), CPI (23), IUML (13), RSP (9), KC (20), PSP (3); NDP (5) separate	Opposition Front: CPI (M) (17), BLD (nil), Janata (6), IUML (Opposition) (3), KC (Pillai) (2), Independent (1)	140
1980	UDF : Cong (I) (17), IUML (14), KC (J) (6), PSP (1), NDP (3), SRP (nil), Janata (5), Independent (1)	LDF: CPI (M) (35), CPI (17), Cong (U) (21), KC (M) (8), KC (P) (1), AIML (5), RSP (6)	140
1982	UDF: Cong (I) (20), Cong (A) (15), KC (M) (6), KC (J) (8), NDP (4), SRP (2), PSP (1), IUML (14), Janata (G) (4), RSP (S) (1), NRSP (nil); DLP (1) separate, Independent (1)	LDF : CPI (M) (26), CPI (13), AIML (4), Cong (S) (7), RSP (4), KC (S) (1), DSP (1), Janata (4), Independents (3)	140
1987	UDF: Cong (I) (33), IUML (15), KC (J) (5), KC (M) (4), NDP (1), CMP (1), Cong (I), Rebel (1), Independents (2)	LDF: CPI (M) (38), CPI (17), Cong (S) (6), RSP (5), Janata (7), LD (1) Independents (Marxist) (4)	140

1991	UDF : Cong (I) (55), IUML (19), KC (M) (10), KC (B) (2), NDP (2), CMP (1), Independent (1)	LDF : CPI (M) (29), CPI (12), JD (3), Cong (S) (2), RSP (2), KC (J) (1), Independent (1)	140
1996	UDF : Cong (I) (37), IUML (13), KC (M) (5), KC (Jacob) (2), JSS (1), Independent (1)	LDF: CPI (M) (41), CPI (18), KC (J) (6), JD (4), RSP (5), Cong (S) (3), Independents (3)	140

The Chief Minister and Cabinet Formation

According to the Constitution and the established parliamentary practice, the leader of the majority party becomes the Chief Minister and forms his Cabinet. As the leader of the party is already known and the party's election machinery revolves around him in normal circumstances, who the next Chief Minister will be in case a particular party is elected to power is already known to the people. But this principle is not always applicable in the context of coalition politics in India. Although the leader of the major party has a claim, he should be acceptable to the other coalition partners too. In the 1987 election to the Kerala Legislative Assembly, the CPI(M) had propagated that K.R. Gowriamma would be the next Chief Minister provided LDF was returned to power. After the elections were over the CPI(M) re-elected E.K. Nayanar as the leader of CPI(M) Parliamentary party. Although the precedence of Nayanar over Gowriamma was the result of the party's internal power relationship, it was generally felt that Nayanar was more acceptable to the LDF partners as the Chief Minister.

There are also instances of minority party leaders becoming the Chief Minister. In Kerala minority party leaders like C. Achutha Menon and P.K. Vasudevan Nair became Chief Ministers in UDF Ministry although both of them belonged to the CPI. The CPI was a partner in UDF during 1970-79. C.H. Muhammed Koya, the leader of Indian Union Muslim League in the 1977-79 Assembly became Chief Minister, although, scarcely for two months, after the exit of Vasudevan Nair's Ministry on 7 October, 1979. But this was a period of political chaos and confusion.

The continuance of the Chief Minister is also dependent on the will of the partners. The third Ministry of K. Karunakaran (1991-95) was under pressure from partners as well as from his own partymen. The Antony faction led by Oommen Chandy took a hostile stand to Karunakaran's leadership of the government. Although rapport had been apparently arrived at between the Karunakaran faction and Antony faction after the general elections in 1987, they fell out again on various issues. The allotment of two Rajya Sabha seats to Karunakaran faction and Muslim League to the exclusion of the candidate of Antony faction was the last straw on the camel's back. Oommen Chandy resigned the post of Finance Minister to be followed by Viswanathan, the Minister for Forests, after sometime. However, the hostility between the factions continued unabated, and the MLAs led by Oommen Chandy turned to the partners for help. With the entry of Muslim League into the fray, supported by Kerala Congress(M) and Kerala Congress(Jacob) the demand for the resignation of Karunakaran became open and strong. After months of infighting between Karunakaran faction on the one hand and Antony faction and the other UDF parties on the other, the Congress High Command intervened to settle the issue. A.K. Antony, Cabinet Minister for Civil Supplies at the Centre, was brought to the State to become the Chief Minister and Karunakaran inducted into the Central Cabinet. There have been earlier instances in Kerala as well as in other States wherein the Congress High Command had interfered in State politics and removed the Chief Ministers. But the removal of Karunakaran is unique, it being the outcome of the joint action of the coalition partners and the anti-Karunakaran faction in the Congress. Had not the partners joined the move against Karunakaran, it would have remained unsuccessful and the resignation of Oommen Chandy infructuous.

With regard to the appointment of Ministers, coalitional politics may create complex situations. Some parties that jointly contest elections may have second thoughts about joining the Cabinet. The Congress which fought the elections together with the CPI, Muslim League, RSP and PSP in 1970 State Assembly elections was in a dilemma whether to join the Ministry or not. They developed the fear of losing the secular image and felt apprehensive that if they joined the Ministry with the Muslim League their prospects in the forthcoming parliamentary elections of 1972 would be adversely affected. A joint meeting of the Kerala Pradesh Congress Committee and the legislature party held at Kochi on 25 February, 1970 decided not to join the government for the time being.[3] But they were prepared to extend support from outside. It was also decided that there would be an extra Cabinet machinery to supervise and control the Ministry. Although the other coalition partners were unhappy about the decision of the Congress, they decided to go ahead with the process of Ministry making.

There was a similar problem with the RSP. The Central Committee of the party had inhibitions about joining the government while the State unit wanted it. So the State unit decided to break away from the party and form an independent Kerala Revolutionary Socialist Party. The PSP got permission from the Central leadership to join the Ministry.

So Ministry making is not automatic after an election. The partners of an election front decide separately on the issue of joining the Ministry. National parties' State units have to consult the national leadership and get their decisions approved.

The Council of Ministers in a coalition government represents a collection of irreconcilable views and even ideologies. Coalitions in Kerala are not often combinations of like-minded parties. They have been often collection of secular and communal parties, socialist and rightist parties, or regional and national parties. But they agree to work on a minimum programme of action, and sometimes the minimum programme is formulated as the election manifesto and got approved by the people.

The nature of coalition politics in Kerala has deprived the Chief Minister of the power of selecting ministers from parties other than his own. It is now established that the coalition partners would choose their own representatives in the Cabinet. In the Achutha Menon Ministry (1970-77), the matter was decided by the coalition parties themselves. A meeting of party leaders held at Kochi on 26 September 1970 decided to leave the right to select ministers to the parties concerned.[4] In another meeting held on 26 November, 1970, party leaders agreed on the ministerial berths to be provided to each party as well as the allocation of Speakership. Accordingly the CPI was to have 3 Ministers in addition to the Chief Minister, the RSP 2, IUML 2 and PSP 1 only. Speakership was allotted to Muslim League and Deputy Speakership to RSP. The Chief Minister had not even participated in these discussions. It is true that he had informally reached an agreement with the non-Congress parties regarding the allocation of ministerial berths. What remained was only an agreement with the Congress which wielded power, although they had decided to remain out of the Ministry.[5]

In the UDF Ministry headed by K. Karunakaran, elected in the general elections of May 1982, the allotment of ministerial berths to different partners was first agreed upon by the Liaison Committee.[6] The selection of individual Ministers was left to the parties concerned. The selection of Ministers was completed in a short time with 19 Ministers sworn in on 24 May, 1982. The strength of the Cabinet had evidently exceeded the strength recommended by the Administrative Commission appointed by the Government of India. The Commission had recommended a size of one-tenth of the total strength of the Lower House. Under the exigency of accommodating all political parties of the UDF the norm was to be deviated from, and all partners were happy about the deviation. This proved that the partners were effective in bargaining for their share in the coalition Ministry, and that the Chief Minister had to make compromises under pressure of coalition politics.

However, in certain circumstances a Chief Minister could effectively check the pressure to include a particular person as Minister. It was in the fourth Ministry of K. Karunakaran (1991-95) that A.K. Antony wanted V.M. Sudheeran to be included as the nominee of Congress (I) Antony faction. V.M. Sudheeran was *persona non grata* for K. Karunakaran as they had bitter fights during his third Ministry when Sudheeran was Speaker of the Legislative Assembly. As Speaker, Sudheeran was just, impartial and assertive, but had occasion to curtail many privileges of the Chief Minister. So Karunakaran opposed tooth and nail the inclusion of V.M. Sudheeran in the Cabinet. A.K. Antony refused to nominate other members of his faction, and Karunakaran had full freedom to choose the representatives of

Antony faction. However, he did not interfere with the nomination of other party members which were decided by the parties themselves.

Distribution of portfolios gives rise to problems. When E.M.S. Namboodiripad formed the seven-party coalition in 1967, the distribution of portfolios was a hard nut to crack. It was the situation of all parties demanding some departments, and none wanting some others. 'Home' and 'Revenue' were the most prestigious portfolios which all parties wanted to lay hands on. 'Food' was repulsive to all. It was a period of acute food shortage in the State and the problem was evidently not going to be solved easily. It was certain that the holder of the portfolio would become the target of attack by all other parties, both in the ruling front and in the opposition.

The CPI(M) offered 'Food' to the CPI and held that food being a matter of national concern it should be handled by a party having national outlook. The CPI could see through the trick and rejected the offer. 'Finance' was also offered to the CPI as an incentive for taking 'Food'. Still the CPI did not take it. Finally, Food portfolio was allotted to the CPI(M) minister K.R. Gowriamma and Finance was given to SSP. Regarding Home portfolio there were protracted negotiations, particularly between CPI(M) and CPI. Being the largest party in the ruling front CPI(M) wanted Home, while the CPI could not relish the idea of CPI(M) holding it. They were afraid that the police force which was under the Home Ministry would be used to suppress them, and as a precaution they demanded it for themselves. However the Chief Minister held his ground and finally allotted Home to one of his own partymen.[7] When 'Labour' was allotted to Mathai Manjooran, leader of Kerala Socialist Party, the CPI and RSP opposed saying that Manjooran was anti-labour in character and that he had participated in the *Vimochana Samaram* that had put an end to the first Communist Ministry. However, the Chief Minister managed to persuade the CPI and RSP to agree to the allotment. RSP staked claim for Public Works, Panchayat and Forests. But only Public Works Department was given to it while Irrigation was separated and given to SSP.

Thus the distribution of portfolios could not be managed easily by Namboodiripad. The Liaison Committee had played a major role in negotiating with the parties and persuading them to be satisfied with less than what they desired. In fact the CPI(M) took the key departments — the Chief Minister, Home, Revenue and Law — and added Transport and Harijan Welfare to them. Its major rival in the front, the CPI, was given three other important portfolios — Agriculture, Industries and Electricity — which could not function effectively without support of the Marxist controlled central departments.

Although the matter was settled for the time, there were continuous demands for the reshuffling of the portfolios. The SSP central leadership raised a demand in May 1967 for a change of portfolios in its favour.[8] They claimed that the allocation of portfolios was neither scientific nor just. The SSP was given Finance but Taxation was separated from it and given to CPI(M) Minister K.R. Gowriamma. The SSP national Chairman S.M. Joshi compared it to "giving him a rubber plantation without the right to tap".[9] Similarly it was claimed that although SSP Minister P.R. Kurup was allotted Irrigation, its administration rested with PWD which was under the RSP. The situation reminded one of the old dyarchy (1919) with Reserved and Transferred subjects and the criticisms raised by Indian leaders against it. SSP leaders pressed for an immediate change. The Chief Minister held discussions with the coalition partners and finally resolved to reject the demands of the SSP. A concession was made by adding a few minor departments like Store Purchase to the Finance department. The Chief Minister did not like the demand for reshuffle at this time and so he used the combined strength of the partners against the SSP claim.

Of course, Food was taken away from Gowriamma in October 1968 and entrusted to Imbichi Bava, another Marxist Minister. But this was only a change among CPI(M) Ministers and was considered an internal affair of the CPI(M). When allegations were raised against ISP Finance Minister P.K. Kunju, the Chief Minister ordered a judicial probe and asked him to resign, taking over the Finance portfolio himself. But there was the practice of the Ministers handing over charge of office to their own party colleagues without the consent of the Chief

Minister. It was pointed out that the IUML Minister Ahmed Kurikal had handed over his portfolio to his party colleague C.H. Muhammed Koya when the former went on leave. The Chief Minister was not consulted when this was done.[10]

In the Achutha Menon Ministry the distribution of portfolios was the work of the Liaison Committee. Achutha Menon himself announced publicly that the decision on the matter would be taken by the Liaison Committee.[11] Nevertheless, being the chairman of the Liaison Committee, he had a role to play in persuading the partners to arrive at a decision. Further, Cabinet formation and distribution of portfolios went through several phases in the Menon Ministry. The Congress had decided at first to remain out of the Cabinet and when the elections to the Lok Sabha were over in March 1971 the State unit of the party thought of joining the Cabinet. Within a month the Congress MLAs passed a resolution in favour of joining the Cabinet although some of the Congress MLAs belonging to the youth section of the party preferred to maintain the *status quo*. Subsequently, a compromise was reached within the party according to which there was to be no immediate entry into the Cabinet, but the Congress Parliamentary board would decide when time was ripe for the Congress to join the Cabinet.[12] Soon after some developments in the Socialist parties compelled the Chief Minister to invite the Congress into the Ministry.

During the time of the Achutha Menon Ministry the SSP was in the opposition and PSP in the ruling front in Kerala. But the merger of SSP and PSP at the national level had its repercussions on Kerala politics. The Kerala Unit of PSP split into three factions: one faction led by Attingal Gopala Pillai, another by N.K. Balakrishnan and a third by D. Damodaran Potti. While the first faction joined the opposition the other factions remained with the ruling front. Still there was uncertainty about the loyalty of these groups. So Achutha Menon informed the Prime Minister Indira Gandhi that it was time for the Congress to join the Ministry. The KPCC decided to join the Ministry on getting consent of the party high command.[13]

There was one more hurdle. There arose a controversy regarding the size of the Cabinet. The Congress preferred a small Cabinet, but the other parties in the ruling front were not prepared to reduce their strength in the Cabinet. Negotiations went on for about three months before a compromise formula was devised. According to the formula the Cabinet was to be expanded from nine to thirteen. The Congress was to have five ministers, and the CPI, the Chief Minister's party, had to drop one of its own. Moreover the CPI had an internal problem. Two of its stalwarts T.V. Thomas and M.N. Govindan Nair, who had been exonerated from corruption charges by an inquiry Commission by this time, had to be included in the Cabinet. Hence three CPI Ministers were dropped, and T.V. Thomas and M.N. Govindan Nair were inducted along with the five Congress Ministers. The new Ministers were sworn in on 23 September, 1971.[14] Portfolios were reallotted. The Congress took Finance from the CPI and Home from the IUML — two most powerful Ministries. As a return gesture, the Congress decided not to press for a Deputy Chief post or the Industries portfolio.

There were some subsequent changes in the Ministry, on account of the induction of the Kerala Congress and replacement of individual Ministers for personal reasons or the death of a Minister. In all these cases, the Chief Minister's role in deciding the size of the Cabinet or the allocation of portfolios was minimal. The individual Ministers including those of the CPI were nominees of the parties concerned.

In the Karunakaran Ministry formed in 1982 the list of Ministers was prepared quickly without any hitch. The Ministers were evidently nominees of the parties themselves. But the total strength of the Ministry had risen to 19 so as to accommodate more aspirants. But the distribution of portfolios was not that simple. There was hard bargaining. The IUML leader C.H. Mohammed Koya insisted on the Deputy Chief Ministership and secured the Industries Ministry for his IUML colleague. The two Kerala Congresses (Mani and Joseph factions) insisted on retaining the portfolios they had held in the previous Ministry.[15] Ultimately the Congress was the biggest loser. However decisions regarding the allocations of positions and portfolios were made in the Liaison Committee, and not by the Chief Minister.

Although K. Karunakaran was submissive enough to accept decisions of the Liaison Committee and of the coalition partners at the initial stage of Cabinet making, later developments proved that he wanted to assert himself as the leader of the Cabinet. The Karunakaran Cabinet underwent several reshuffles owing to infighting in the coalition parties, but two reshuffles were serious and affected the Congress party itself.

Cabinet Management

Ministries once formed do not remain so until the end. They are expanded, reshuffled or sometimes Ministers dropped. These are actions taken by the Chief Minister in managing the Council of Ministers and controlling their portfolios. But these actions are not as easily taken as in a single-party government, for there is threat that the offended partners may withdraw support anytime.

Some instances of such situations that have arisen during coalition Ministries in Kerala may be examined below. In May 1967, during the first coalition Ministry under E.M.S. Namboodiripad, the SSP leaders demanded a change of portfolios in their favour.[16] The Chief Minister held discussions with the coalition partners regarding this demand, and with their backing could reject the demand of SSP.[17] Later on he made some changes under pressure from the CPI.[18] Thus Namboodiripad could show his dexterity in dealing with similar cases differently according to circumstances.

When some corruption charges were levelled against a few of his colleagues he was forced to meet a new situation. He ordered a *prima facie* case inquiry into the cases against P.K. Kunju with the concurrence of the Liaison Committee, while he could do it in the case of M.K. Krishnan and B. Wellington without the same. However, it must be admitted that P.K. Kunju belonged to a different party while M.K. Krishnan belonged to his own party the CPI(M) and B. Wellington to the KTP which was a close ally of the CPI(M). Following the *prima facie* inquiry the Chief Minister gave a clean chit to the latter two while he ordered further probe into the case of P.K. Kunju. This differential treatment, however justifiable from the point of view of the CPI(M), had caused resentment among the partners, particularly the CPI.

While the CPI(M) claimed that the Chief Minister had power to remove Ministers including those of the other parties, CPI and ISP held that he had no such right regarding Ministers of other parties. The situation arose when Namoodiripad alleged that T.V. Thomas, CPI Minister, was conspiring with the enemies of the United Front to topple the government. Although this was interpreted as an expression of lack of confidence on the part of the Chief Minister, the latter refused to resign and questioned the right of the Chief Minister to express such lack of confidence in a coalitional set-up.[19] On this question of whether the Chief Minister of a coalition had the right to demand the resignation of a Minister, Namboodiripad did not seem to be steady and held different views on different occasions.

Namboodiripad seemed to ignore the coalitional character of his government and ignored the concerned parties while taking decisions. For instance, he did not bother to consult the ISP, the party of P.K. Kunju, before instituting an inquiry into charges of corruption.

Achutha Menon's second Ministry formed after the Assembly election in September 1970 consisted of only four parties — CPI, RSP, PSP and IUML — and the Congress only offered support from outside. The Chief Minister did not play any role in the formation of this Cabinet; the selection of Ministers and the distribution of portfolios were left to the decision of the Liaison Committee. The decision of the Congress to join the Ministry later in July 1971 necessitated its expansion and a redistribution of portfolios. While the Congress preferred a small Cabinet, none of the other partners liked to have a cut on their representation. It was through a prolonged discussion between the partners that a compromise formula was reached at length. Although Achutha Menon played the key role in persuading the Congress to join the Ministry, he had no role in the selection of Ministers including those of his own party.

Now it is established that the Ministers of a coalition Cabinet shall be chosen by the parties themselves. Probably the Chief Minister can play a more important role in the selection of Ministers from his own party than of the other Ministers. This applies to expansion and removal also. Recently when the Janata Dal decided to replace Neelalohithadasan Nadar consequent on a "sex scandal", the Chief Minister E.K. Naynar kept a discreet silence over the whole affair and treated the matter as if it was an internal matter of the party concerned.[20]

Factional fights in the ruling parties particularly the Congress(I), Kerala Congress, RSP, etc. had led to the demand for change of Ministers or of portfolios. Chief Ministers themselves had led factional feuds, as exemplified by Karunakaran who was chiefly instrumental for removing Vayalar Ravi from the Home Ministry in 1986.[21] As regards factional fights of other parties Chief Minister's have generally taken a policy of co-existence through non-interference.

Liaison Committees

Coalitions in Kerala — both ruling and opposition — have come to accept the importance of co-ordination committees in cementing the relation between allies. The CPI(M)-led coalition under Namboodiripad was the first to form a co-ordination committee in the State. Earlier coalitions had not thought that such a device would help strengthen the relationship. The committee was composed of one representative each of the constituent parties and was presided over by the Chief Minister *ex officio.*[22] There was no strict rule regarding the number of members, and very often special invitees also attended the meetings. The committee was not a compact body and the discussions were not often free and full. It was the co-ordination committee that later came to be called Liaison Committee in Kerala. Although it had a convener, it had no secretariat or office; nor were any minutes kept strictly.[23] In the absence of proper recording of decisions taken, there were occasional disputes and the members tended to interpret decisions to suit their interests. This situation sometimes rendered the Chief Ministers bold enough to ignore the committee. Indeed the CPI(M) party machinery always wanted to keep control of the Liaison Committee during its tenures and was not prepared to give any independent role to it.

There were a number of other factors that stood in the way of strengthening the Liaison Committee:[24] (i) There was no consensus among the coalition partners about the role of the

Committee; (ii) The rivalry between the two Communist parties converted it into a forum for mutual fighting; (iii) The inability of the Chief Minister to play the role of an honest broker led to the growth of groupism in the Committee; (iv) On many occasions the decisions taken by the Committee were flouted by the front partners, particularly the CPI(M); and (v) Policy questions were sometimes not referred to the Committee before they were presented to the Cabinet. Thus although started with good intentions, the Liaison Committee could not work as desired, and by mid-1969 the Committee ceased to meet.

During the Achutha Menon Ministry (1970-77) the Liaison Committee functioned more effectively than before. A number of factors contributed to the effective functioning of the Committee during this period.[25] The most important among them were that (i) the Chief Minister himself wanted the Committee to be a respectable body, and (ii) the razor-thin majority of the coalition compelled the ruling front to stay together or face a collapse. However, after the inclusion of the Congress in the Ministry, the Committee had a chequered career and the Congress was accused of hegemonistic tendencies.

On the whole the Achutha Menon regime was the golden era of the Co-ordination Committee. In the matter of selection of Ministers and distribution of portfolios as well as in resolving political conflicts, the Committee played a more powerful role than the Chief Minister or the Cabinet. Towards the end of 1972 there were reports about the helplessness of the Chief Minister Achutha Menon in running the government owing to the iron grip of the Committee.

In 1980 the LDF government adopted a more elaborate structure for its committee. A three-tier organisational set-up was accepted with a 21-member State committee, 7 member secretariat and committees at the district and constituency levels[26].

During the UDF Ministry (1982-87) headed by K. Karunakaran, there was a change in the composition of the Co-ordination Committee. It was made a loose and large body with 35 to 50 members. There was also to be an executive body consisting of the convener and one representative each from the coalition partners. The idea of Co-ordination Committee was extended to district level also, each district having Committee with four members from each party, to promote co-operation among coalition partners at the lower levels. Thus co-ordination was supposed to disseminate to lower levels theoretically although not functioning effectively at the top. The State Level Committee was powerful in the first two years of the Karunakaran regime, as it could play a decisive role in the distribution of seats among the allies, and in the preparation of election manifesto for the mid-term elections of 1982. After the 1982 elections, the Committee could monitor the formation of the Ministry, the distribution of portfolios, the preparation of the programme of the budget session and even the transfer of government officials including the Chief Secretary.[27]

In course of time the Committee became ineffective. As criticism arose about the inefficiency of the Committee from the part of the allies, it was decided to restructure it with a three-tier system. In January 1984 the Co-ordination Committee was reconstituted to include: (i) a general committee with four representatives each from the constituent parties; (ii) an executive committee with two representatives each; and (iii) a steering committee having nine members with the deputy leader of the Congress(I) legislature party as convener and the Chief Minister as the chairman.[28] It was held that the steering committee being a compact body would be able to take immediate action to resolve problems facing the front. The new arrangement worked for some time, but the various committees soon got into the whirlpool of factional feuds.

The successive governments after 1987 — Naynar's second LDF Ministry (1987-91), UDF Ministry (1991-96) and Naynar's third LDF Ministry (1996-2001) — also have functioned with the help of Co-ordination Committees. It is now accepted that no coalition government can function without a committee to co-ordinate the ruling allies. The powers and position of the committee have varied from time to time; sometimes its powers have waxed and sometimes waned in relation to the Chief Minister and the Cabinet. Although it cannot be considered a super-Cabinet, it occasionally gives strong directives to the Cabinet on policy matters particularly when controversies are involved. There are recent instances of the LDF State Committee (State Level Liaison Committee of the ruling LDF) discussing hike in bus fares, seats in professional colleges, granting plus-two schools, etc.[29] The conflict that arose in the LDF on the question of Rajya Sabha seats on the eve of the Rajya Sabha elections in June 2000 was also settled formally on the floor of the LDF Committee.[30] Nevertheless there is dissatisfaction among the allies about the big brotherly attitude of the CPI(M) toward the allies and of the negligence shown by the government about meeting of the Co-ordination Committee.[31]

It is interesting to note that not only the ruling alliance but also the opposition alliance maintain co-ordination committees. The UDF which is in the opposition today makes use of the UDF State committee, district and constituency committees for co-ordinating the allied parties at various levels. The UDF State committee discusses problems of their common concern and prepare strategy for solving them. The decision to offer Rajya Sabha seat to Muslim League in the June 2000 election was discussed in several rounds of the State committee's meetings and finally resolved in the committee.[32]

Coalition Chief Ministers

The above analysis of Cabinet formation and management has thrown light on another variable of coalition politics, the personality of the Chief Minister. It is needless to say that the personal characteristics and leadership styles of Chief Ministers differ. One may be assertive, dominating and more concerned about one's image-building than about the image of his Cabinet or of his colleagues. Another may be self-effacing, unauthoritarian and prepared to respect colleagues and the borders of their authority. A third type may be of a partyman, partisan in approach, committed to his party and prepared to sacrifice the government in the interests of his party. There may be other types too as each Chief Minister is *sui generis.* None of the coalition Chief Ministers in Kerala since 1960 — Pattom A. Thanu Pillai, E.M.S. Namboodiripad, C. Achutha Menon, K. Karunakaran. A.K. Antony and E.K. Naynar — can be clubbed together into the same personality model. Some characteristic or other may be predominant in each one.

Pattom A. Thanu Pillai, a prominent freedom fighter of former Travancore and the first Chief Minister (officially designated Prime Minister) of Travancore under the Travancore Interim Constitution Act, 1948, immediately after Independence, was generally considered very authoritarian in his approach to governance. It was his lack of regard for colleagues that antagonised the latter and led to the fall of his Ministries.

E.M.S. Namboodiripad, one of the builders of the CPI and later of the CPI(M) in India in general and Kerala in particular was a Marxist theoretician of a very high intellectual calibre. He was also a political strategist having been responsible for the coalition experiments in the State under the leadership of Marxist party. The first single-party government under him (1957-59) fell under the impact of the *Vimochana Samaram* led by the communal forces in the State. The coalition government under him (1967-69) also lasted only for about two and a half years as it broke owing to dissensions within the coalition. As the leader of a heterogeneous coalition, he failed in keeping it intact by the art of persuasion and a policy of fair treatment. He often appeared as a party leader who sought to make the maximum pay off for his own party. So he failed to command respect of his colleagues who accused him of 'big brother' attitude. Occasionally he ignored the coalitional set-up and took decisions on his own despite the existence of a Liaison Committee. He used different criteria in dealing with colleagues and failed to give them an equal treatment. He also could not show much imagination in handling difficult situations like the food supply crisis, break down of law and order owing to the growth of gheraos and anti-Centre agitations.

C. Achutha Menon was perhaps the most effective in controlling and co-ordinating a coalition government. He had a vision about the Chief Minister's role and powers in a coalition Cabinet. According to him, the duty of the Chief Minister was to ensure the harmonious functioning of the Ministry while at the same time ensuring discipline.[33] This is as much true of coalition governments as of single-party governments, but developing proper relationships between the Ministers themselves as between the Ministers and the Chief Minister is the most difficult task for a coalition Chief Minister. He conceived of his role as that of a moderator; that of a first among equals and not of the big brother.

He was prepared to leave the choice of his colleagues and their portfolios to the coalition parties themselves and to the Co-ordination Committee. This clarity of vision enabled Menon to play a moderating role whenever there was inter-party or intra-party conflicts in the coalition. Decisions regarding other departments were taken only with the consent of the Ministers concerned.

Moreover, his gentle and soft-spoken behaviour, buttressed by the integrity of character and political credibility made him always acceptable to his colleagues and other partymen. According to Sanjivayya, former President of Indian National Congress, Achutha Menon was a "gentleman of integrity and constructive vision".[34] He was prepared to use the same standards to all ministers whenever some allegations of corruption came up and he issued orders of inquiry immediately even if his own partymen were involved. He kept himself on a low profile, but was stern in dealing with pressure groups whether they were state employees, teachers or college managements or the like. Sense and sensibility combined in him sweetly making him affable and accessible to the high and the low.

K. Karunakaran, a veteran Congress leader of long parliamentary experience, has had the right claim to be the chief of a Congress-led coalition. He became Chief Minister four times but he could not complete all terms. During the terms that he completed fully (1982-87) or nearly fully (1991-95) his performance was not satisfactory to all allies or even to his own partymen. During the first-half of his completed term (1982-87), he remained moderately ambitious and relied more on consent and compromise.[35] Ministerial positions and portfolios were distributed among partners through agreements reached mainly with the help of the Co-ordination Committee. Individual ministers were nominated by the concerned parties themselves, and intra-coalition relations went on smoothly. During the second-half, Karunakaran started to assert himself and ignored the arrangements made for reaching consent and compromise. He had stage-managed a Cabinet reshuffle in 1986 and pushed out Ministers whom he regarded as rivals. The exit of Vayalar Ravi, his own partyman, from Ministry and the transfer of Finance from K.M. Mani, the leader of Kerala Congress (M) were the results of this reshuffling.[36] During his next term

(1991-95) he proved himself a more vigourous faction leader rather than a leader of government. He had even tried to engineer splits within some of the coalition partners by his crafty techniques. Personal hostility to him led to the creation of several factions within his party, the Congress(I). This culminated in these factions joining together with the coalition allies to remove him from the Chief Ministership. In spite of his hold on the party high command in Delhi, he was compelled to hand over power to A.K. Antony, the leader of the strongest anti-Karunakaran faction in the party, one year before the completion of his term.

A.K. Antony, an idealist to the core, has often appeared to be unwilling to take power as Chief Minister. Although the leader of a faction in the Congress(I), he shows the tendency to rise above the faction when in power. As coalition Chief Minister he has shown a policy of non-interference toward other parties and their portfolios, and he has shown respect to the Co-ordination Committee as an essential institution of coalition government. His self-effacting transparency has made him considerably acceptable to the allies.

E.K. Naynar has the longest innings as Chief Minister, having been able to ride rather smoothly through two terms (1987-91, 1996-2001), although he had difficulties during the first term (1980-81). Despite occasional complaints from the allies about not convening the Co-ordination Committee and the big brother attitude of the CPI(M), he has been successful in humouring the allies as well as in keeping control over the rivals in his party. He maintains the policy of strict non-interference with the departments of allies as also with their internal feuds. His personal style of making biting remarks and his funny conduct have politically cushioned off several traumas.

NOTES

1. P. John John, *Coalition Governments in Kerala* (Thiruvananthapuram, 1983), p. 75.
2. N. Jose Chander, *The Socio-economic and Political Background of the Members of the Eighth Kerala Legislative Assembly – A Report* (mimeograph) (Thiruvananthapuram 1992), p. 2.
3. *Malayala Manorama* (Kottayam), 26 September 1970.
4. *Malayala Manorama* (Kottayam), 27 September 1970.

5. A.A. Sebastian, *Role of Chief Minister in Coalition Governments: A Study of Kerala* (Ph.D. Thesis submitted to the University of Kerala, Thiruvananthapuram) 1994, p. 133.
6. *The Hindu* (Coimbatore), 24 May 1982.
7. K.V. Varghese, *United Front Government in Kerala 1967-69* (Madras, 1978), p. 33.
8. *Indian Express* (Madurai), 15 May 1967.
9. P.K. Kunju and P.R. Kurup joined the Ministry as representatives of SSP. But the SSP soon got split into National SSP and Kerala SSP, and both factions remained in the ruling front. The Ministers were part of Kerala SSP. When the Indian Socialist Party (ISP) was formed in May 1969 the Ministers formally became members of ISP.
10. *The Desabhimani* (Calicut), 17 August 1969.
11. *Malayala Manorama* (Kottayam), 27 September 1970.
12. *Indian Express* (Madurai), 25 April 1971.
13. *Kerala Kaumudi* (Thiruvananthapuram), 4 July 1971.
14. *Indian Express* (Madurai), 26 September 1971.
15. *India Today,* Vol.7, No. 11, 15 June 1982, p. 27.
16. *Indian Express* (Madurai), 15 May 1967.
17. "Cross Currents in Kerala", *Economic and Political Weekly,* Vol. II, No. 1, 24 Jan. 1967, p. 115.
18. A.A. Sebastian, n.(5), p.76.
19. *Indian Express* (Madurai), 12 June 1968.
20. *Kalakaumudi* (Malayalam), 20 February 2000.
21. *The Hindu* (Coimbatore), 18 April 1986.
22. T.J. Nossiter, *Communism in Kerala: A Study in Political Adaptation* (New Delhi, 1982), p. 274.
23. Azheekodan Raghavan, a prominent CPI(M) leader, was the first convenor.
24. A.A. Sebastian, n. (5), pp. 319-21.
25. *Ibid.*, p. 327.
26. A. Balakrishnan Nair, *The Government and Politics of Kerala,* (Thiruvananthapuram, 1994), p. 276.
27. *Kerala Kaumudi* (Thiruvananthapuram), 2 June 1982.
28. A A. Sebastian, n.(5), p. 339.
29. *The Hindu* (Thiruvananthapuram), October 1999; The *Mathorubhumi* (Kottayam), 2 March 2000.
30. *The Hindu* (Thiruvananthapuram), 17 June 2000.
31. *The Mathrubhumi* (Kottayam), 10 February 2000.
32. *The Hindu,* 12 June 2000.
33. C. Achutha Menon, "Coalition Government, the Kerala Experience", in R. Prasannan (ed), *Twenty-five Years of Kerala Legislature* (Thiruvananthapuram, 1983), p. 85.
34. *The Link,* New Delhi; 26 September1971, p. 14.
35. A.A. Sebastian, n.(5), p. 237.
36. *The Hindu* (Coimbatore), 14 May 1986, 17 May 1986.

5

COALITION POLITICS IN WEST BENGAL

Coalition politics emerged in West Bengal after the general elections of 1967. Although two leftist alliances were pitted against the Congress in this election they had visualised the possibility of a coalition government after the elections. The decade from 1967 to 1977 was a period of experimentation with coalition politics and was characterised by political instability. After 1977 a single CPI(M) dominated coalition of Left parties fought the elections against the Congress(I) and won majority throughout. Thus a coalition of parties achieved stability and came to dominate West Bengal politics, with no party being able to provide an alternative government.

In the 1967 Assembly elections, the Left parties having failed to come together under a common roof emerged into two combinations. They were: the People's United Left Front (PULF) and the United Left Front (ULF). Thus there were two fronts fighting against the Congress(I).

Results of the Assembly Elections of 1967

Total number of seats	-	280
Congress(I)	-	127
PULF		
Bangla Congress	-	34
Communist Party of India	-	16
Forward Bloc	-	13
Praja Socialist Party	-	7
Lok Sevak Sangh	-	5
Gorkha League	-	2
Bolshevik Party	-	0
ULF		
Communist Party of India (Marxist)	-	43

Samyukta Socialist Party	-	7
Revolutionary Socialist Party	-	6
Socialist Unity Centre	-	4
Workers' Party	-	2
Revolutionary Communist Party	-	2
Forward Bloc (Marxist)	-	1
Independents	-	10
Others		
Jan Sangh	-	1
Swatantra	-	1

The Congress had dominated West Bengal politics from the first general elections in 1952 to the elections in 1967, but dissidence in the two strongest parties — the Congress and the Communists — led to the division of the parties and to new political alignments. The dissident groups — the Bangla Congress of the Indian National Congress and the CPI (M) of the Communist Party of India — turned out to be the most vote-capturing parties of the opposition in the 1967 elections. It was the idea of presenting a united opposition that influenced the considerations of the various political parties and drove them to the formation of electoral alliances against the Congress. The 1967 elections witnessed the downfall of the Congress and the victory of non-Congress electoral fronts, viz. ULF and PULF, who combined to form a coalition government. The Congress, although the largest party, had no promising leader, and having lost the prominent leaders at the hustings decided not to stake its claim. The new United Front of 14 parties formed the first coalition Ministry in West Bengal on 3 March, 1967 under Ajoy Mukherjee, leader of the Bangla Congress, as Chief Minister. Jyoti Basu, CPI(M) leader, became Deputy Chief Minister and Minister for Finance and Transports. The Ministry consisted of 18 members[1] : Bangla Congress – 3; CPI(M) – 3; CPI – 2; FB – 2; RSP – 1; SUC – 1; SSP – 1; Workers' Party – 1; Gorkha League – I; PSP – 1; LSS – 1 and Independent – 1. The UF adopted an 18-point programme based on which they sought to eradicate all anti-social acts committed under the Congress rule.

This Ministry could not last beyond one year. Internal rivalries and external developments like Naxalite activities, tension in the industrial sector and the spate of gheraos in which ministers themselves were targeted led to political realignments.[2] There was an effort from various quarters to pressurise Ajoy Mukherjee to resign and form an alternative Ministry excluding the Communists. As it did not materialise, the attention turned to P.C. Ghosh, the Food Minister, who resigned and formed the Progressive Democratic Front with the Congress. After some dramatic developments, the Governor Dharam Vira dismissed the UF government. A new government was formed by P.C. Ghosh as Chief Minister and supported by the Congress. The Ghosh Ministry came to an end after four months when President's rule was imposed in the State one year after the fourth general elections.

The President's rule offered a period of quiet after a nightmare of violence in politics. However, massive defections and the rise of new parties became the order of the day during this period. A 'third force' threatened to emerge on a Congress-UF axis around a group of defectors from the Bangla Congress.[3] This led to further split of the Congress from which a section headed by Jehangir Kabir broke away and formed the Bangiya Jatiya Dal (National Party of Bengal). P.C. Ghosh who had by this time worked out an alliance with Humayun Kabir and formed the West Bengal unit of Lok Dal parted company and rejoined the Congress. Besides there was the Indian National Democratic Front formed by Ashutosh Ghosh who was more inclined to the UF than to the Congress.

The mid-term poll was held in February 1969 and the United Front consisting of 14 parties was elected to the Legislative Assembly with a huge majority of 218 out of 280. The partywise breakdown was as follows:

Results of the Assembly Elections of 1969[4]

Total number of seats	-	280
Congress (I)	-	55
CPI (M)	-	80
Bangla Congress	-	33
CPI	-	30
FB	-	21

RSP	-	12
SSP	-	9
SUC	-	7
Gorkha League	-	5
LSS	-	4
PSP	-	5
INDF	-	1
Swatantra	-	0
Jan Sangh	-	0
Independents and others	-	19

The UF included all the Left parties and the Bangla Congress. In accordance with a previous understanding Ajoy Mukherjee was elected leader and the Chief Minister, and Jyoti Basu was appointed Deputy Chief Minister. All the major portfolios were taken by the CPI(M) after hard bargaining. The Ministry of Home was distributed between Ajoy and Basu. On the whole the distribution of portfolios gave the CPI(M) virtual control over the government. The second UF Ministry thus came to be sworn in on 25 February, 1969.

Efforts were made to launch an anti-Centre struggle, and the UF government raised demands like the removal of Governor Dharam Vira, withdrawal of all CRPF forces from the State, etc. There was also a *bandh* sponsored by the Ministry on 10 April 1969 to focus attention on the Centre. But a spate of clashes in certain areas of West Bengal, particularly in districts where the CPI(M) was relatively weak sharpened the intra-Front conflicts.[5] Interestingly enough, the five districts where the CPI(M) was strong — Calcutta, Howrah, Hooghly, Burdwan and North 24 Parganas — were free from such clashes. The police remained silent as violence raged on without restraint. This only reflected the manoeuvres of the CPI(M) to gain control over the politics of the State. The Bangla Congress adopted a resolution which was in fact critical of the UF rule and of the CPI(M). Ajoy Mukherjee, the Chief Minister, went on a hunger strike on 1 December, 1969 in protest against the 'jungle law' and the 'barbarian administration' that prevailed in the State.[6] The Chief Minister and his supporters wanted to shift the Home Ministry from Basu. And some had even thought of a 'mini-front' government without the CPI(M) in it.[7] However, matters did not improve, and Ajoy Mukherjee resigned as Chief Minister on 16 March, 1970, putting an end to the 13-month rule of the second UF Ministry. Basu staked his claim to form the government, being the leader of the largest party. But as the other parties were strongly opposed to the idea, the Governor imposed President's rule on 21 March, 1970. The CPI(M) launched a campaign against President's rule and sought dissolution of the Assembly.

West Bengal continued to have political turmoils. The year 1970 witnessed an upsurge in violent activities and political murders. The CPI(M) was getting isolated from the major partners of the 14-party UF. On the eve of the 1971 elections the UF parties were split into three groups[8] : (i) the Six-Party Combination headed by the CPI (M) and comprising, in addition, the Workers' party, RCPI, FB (Marxist), Bolshevik Party and the Biplabi Bangla Congress which had broken out in rebellion against the Bangla Congress' official policy of sympathy with the Congress; (ii) the Eight-Party Combination headed by the CPI and comprising, in addition, the Forward Bloc, SSP, SUC, Gorkha League, a RCPI faction (Anadi Das group) and Bolshevik Party along with a section of PSP; (iii) Bangla Congress which stood aloof from both the above combinations. The Bangla Congress tried to forge a grand electoral alliance with the Congress (R), but as the latter suspected them of having links with the Congress (O) the alliance did not come off. The Congress (R) and Congress (O) preferred to fight independently. As a result there was a five-cornered contest among the ULF, ULDF, Bangla Congress, Cong(R) and Cong(O) in March 1971. The election results were favourable to the CPI(M)-led combination.

Results of the Assembly Election, 1971[9]

Congress (R)	-	105	PSP	-	3
Congress (O)	-	2	RSP	-	3
Bangla Congress	-	5	Gorkha League	-	2
CPI (M)	-	111	Jarkhand	-	2
RCPI	-	3	Muslim League	-	7
FB (M)	-	2	Jan Sangh	-	1

Workers' Party	-	2	INDF	-	3
Biplabi Bangla Cong.	-	2			
Bolshevik Party	-	0			
CPI	-	13			
FB	-	3			
SSP	-	1			
SUC	-	7			
			Total	-	**277**

Elections had been countermanded in three seats.

The CPI(M) which had the largest number of seats in the Assembly staked claim to form the government. Jyoti Basu who was elected leader of the 125 member ULF wrote to the Governor pressing his claim.[10] The Governor refused to meet him. All the ULDF parties except the SUC decided to support a coalition which would include the Congress (R).[11] The SUC was in favour of a coalition between ULF and ULDF. But the Congress(R) decided to join a government headed by Ajoy Mukherjee, the Bangla Congress leader. A "Democratic Coalition" was subsequently formed by six parties — Congress (R), Bangla Congress, Muslim League, Gorkha League, a PSP faction and a SSP faction — and headed by Ajoy Mukherjee. CPI and FB extended support from outside. Thus a twenty-five member non-Marxist democratic coalition Ministry was sworn in on 2 April, 1971. The Ministry's composition reflected as much of Congress domination as the 1969 Ministry was Marxist dominated, having allotted to the non-Congress participants only a slender margin of portfolios.[12]

The weakness of the Ministry was exposed when a no-confidence motion moved by Jyoti Basu was passed on 15 May 1971 by 132-141 votes.[13] The CPI(M) was still not called to form the government. President's rule was again clamped down on the State on 29 June, 1971, hardly three months after the formation of the Democratic Coalition government.[14] During the President's rule this time, the Central Government began to take direct interest in the matters of West Bengal, and created a new Cabinet post of West Bengal Affairs Minister to deal exclusively with the problems of the State. Sidhartha Sankar Ray the Central Minister for Education, was assigned the new post as an additional duty.[15] The motivation behind the new development was obviously to undo the CPI(M) influence in the State administration as well as to boost up the morale of the Congress workers. The Congress prestige was further raised by India's victory in the war for Bangladesh liberation in 1971.

But the law and order in the State was deteriorating. Naxalite killings increased and there were instances of political prisoners beaten to death while in confinement.[16] People began agitating for fresh elections, and it could not be deferred indefinitely.

The next polls were conducted in March 1972. One conspicuous feature of the election was the alliance between the Congress(R) and the CPI-led ULDF. They had formed the Progressive Democratic Alliance in order to fight the "forces of right reaction, left adventurism and disruption".[17] Thus there were two fronts only — the PDA and the ULF. There were allegations of large scale rigging and corruption under the direction of the Central authorities. The PDA swept the polls with a huge majority. In the political process preceding the election some parties like the Bangla Congress, SSP and PSP had merged with the Congress (R) and disappeared while some others failed to win a single seat in the election.

Results of the Assembly Elections, 1972

Congress (R)	-	216
Congress (O)	-	2
CPI	-	35
CPI (M)	-	14
SUC	-	1
RSP	-	3
Workers' Party	-	1
Independents and others	-	8
Total	-	**280**

Sidhartha Sankar Ray was unanimously elected leader of the PDA and Biswanath Mukherjee, leader of the CPI legislature party, was elected as the deputy leader. S.S. Ray was invited to form the government and a Congress Ministry took office on 20 March, 1972 with 28 Ministers. The CPI supported the government from outside. Ray declared that his government would serve as "a workers' government, a peasants' government and a government of the people". Within a couple of months rupture appeared in the Congress-CPI alliance, when the CPI executive committee accused a section of Congress workers of trying to expand their area of influence.[18] In fact a large section of Congressmen were opposed to the coalition and had found the PDA irrelevant once the election was won.

Efforts were made to improve the relations between the two parties by effecting better co-ordination.[19] For this purpose, an Assembly Co-ordination Committee was suggested consisting of members from both parties. It was also suggested to form a consultative committee for each department of government consisting of MLAs drawn from both parties. Nevertheless the working of Congress-CPI alliance remained a far cry in the post-election situation. It was alleged that the Congress-led Ministry tended to introduce bills without consulting the CPI.[20] The Congress accused the CPI of 'hunting with the hound and running with the hare'.

In July 1973, the CPI planned a *bandh* to protest against the price hike of essential commodities. The CPI (M) also organised a separate *bandh* the same day, and both parties claimed credit for its success. Since then there were efforts to bring the CPI and the CPI (M) together in a united movement against hoarders, profiteers and black marketers. The Progressive Democratic Alliance formally came to an end in June 1974, after two years and three months of the formation of the Congress Ministry in March 1972.

Since 1974 political developments in the country led to a reclustering of political forces in the State as well as at the Centre. The inflow of refugees from Bangladesh after its liberation continued. The rise in the price of crude oil together with heavy expenditure on the part of government had an inflationary effect on the State's economy. The Proclamation of Emergency in the country on 26 June, 1975 in the wake of the Allahabad High Court judgement invalidating the election of Indira Gandhi and the police excesses following it led to further unpopularity of the Congress.

It was in these circumstances that the Janata party was elected to power at the Centre in the Lok Sabha elections held in

March 1977. The Janata government decided to dissolve the Legislative Assemblies of nine States including West Bengal where the Congress party had suffered a crushing defeat at the Lok Sabha polls. The Central decision was opposed by the West Bengal government led by Congress(R) which planned a *satyagraha* in protest as well as by six other States which sought to move the Supreme Court. The Supreme Court rejected the petition on 30 April, 1977 and the then acting President B.D. Jatti ordered dissolution of the State Assemblies.

The election to the West Bengal Legislative Assembly in 1977 was mainly a triangular contest between the Janata party, the Congress(R) and the Left Front comprising CPI(M), FB, FB(M), RSP, RCPI and the Biplabi Bangla Congress. CPI, SUCI and others fought independently. There were moves to form an alliance between Janata and CPI(M), but no agreement could be reached as the Janata insisted on a larger share of seats than what the CPI(M) would offer.[21] However, the CPI(M) could, surprisingly to themselves, win a sweeping victory.

Results of the Assembly Elections, 1977[22]

Left Front:	CPI (M)	-	178
	FB	-	25
	RSP	-	20
	RCPI	-	3
	BBC	-	1
	FB (M)	-	3
		-	**230**
Others:	Congress (R)	-	20
	Janata	-	29
	CPI	-	2
	SUCI	-	4
	CPI (M-L)	-	1
	Muslim League	-	1
	Congress for Democracy	-	2
	Gorkha League	-	2
	Independents	-	2
		-	**63**

Out of the total number of 294 seats in the Assembly, elections were held only to 293 seats.

The new government took office on 21 June, 1977 under CPI(M) leader Jyoti Basu as Chief Minister. It pledged to carry out the governance of the State on a 36-point programme following the spirit of the 32-point programme of the second United Front government. The superior strength of the CPI(M) within the coalition made it virtually a single-party government. The other partners, no longer being indispensible, were bound to toe the line of the CPI(M) in regard to matters of policy and ideology. However, the coalition was strengthened since 1980 with the inclusion of CPI and some other small parties. The Left Front government under Basu could work successfully in solving several problems that arose from land reforms, influx of refugees from Bangladesh and devastating floods. However, Basu realised in the first three years of his government that running a Communist government within a capitalist framework called for drastic adjustments.[23] In 1979 Basu observed that coalition governments would continue to be useful in West Bengal and the country as a whole for some more time to come.[24] It was prophetic as Left Front continued to win successive elections in two decades after 1977.

In 1982 elections the CPI(M) won 174 seats out of 294.[25] The Left Front secured a total strength of 238 members together with the allies. The Janata almost disappeared, and State politics was polarised between the Congress and the Marxists.

In 1987, in spite of Rajiv Gandhi's personal attack on Basu, the Left Front secured more seats than in 1982. The CPI(M) won 187 seats and the Front partners — CPI, RSP, FB, West Bengal Socialist Party and others — together brought in 64 seats, adding the strength to a total of 251. The opposition was weak. The Congress (I) had 40 seats, SUCI had 2 and Muslim League 1.[26] In 1991 the CPI(M) alone got 186 seats and the LF together got 246 out of 294. The Congress(I) had got 41 members. In 1996 elections there was a decline of CPI(M) popularity. The CPI(M) got 158 seats only and the LF together 204 out of 294 Assembly seats.

Coalition Management

The Left-dominated coalition politics in West Bengal since 1977 has provided a unique experience of political stability. It has provided an unbroken continuity in politics and policy with a commitment to popular land reforms and industrial progress. There have been differences of opinion regarding political issues among the Left coalition partners and they have often come to clashes threatening to break the coalition. But they some how soon reached a compromise and this was facilitated by the ideological nearness that the Left parties in general possess.

Atul Kohli says that the success in CPI(M)'s effective strategy for governance can be partly explained by the change in ideology.[27] The party became prepared to give up its traditional antipathy towards parliamentary institutions and to cherish the values of democracy. It became prepared to shed the militant techniques like gheraos and land grab movements of the pre-1977 decade and replace them by legal and constitutional struggles. The party was also willing to replace its class criteria by political standards in identifying its friends and enemies, and welcomed nearly all social classes into the party fold. The new commitment to reformism made the CPI(M) more of a social democratic party and less of a traditional Communist party. The CPI(M) has also consolidated a coalition of middle and lower strata by implementing some modest redistributive program-mmes.[28] The CPI (M) changed its traditional policy toward the industrial capitalists and welcomed multinational industries to West Bengal. There were some feeble protests from the coalition partners in the Left Front Co-ordination Committee as early as 6 January1978 against the tendency to rely on the multinationals too much.[29] Such dissent was ignored, and Jyoti Basu went ahead welcoming industrialists from whatever quarters they were willing to come.

However, such dissent re-appeared in later years when Basu made a restatement of the Industrial Policy in the Legislative Assembly in 1994.[30] RSP and FB demanded a "proper debate" among the Front partners before the Industrial Policy was finally framed. They were of the view that Basu's outline was not substantially different from the Centre's new economic policy. Massive protests were organised through strike by nearly a million workers and employees in the organised industry and services on 29 September, 1994, and this was preceded by mass arrests of the members and sympathisers of the Left parties exceeding one lakh.[31] RSP wanted and was granted a special bipartite meeting with the CPI(M) on the issue, as it was sore that the Left Front had not been consulted about the Industrial Policy. The meeting assuaged RSP's ruffled feelings by incorporating in a joint statement that the State government had been compelled to invite multinational corporations and Indian monopoly business in view of the Centre's discriminatory attitude towards the State during the past three decades.[32] Interestingly enough, the FB which had earlier criticised the policy statement did not seek one-to-one meeting with the CPI(M) leadership and, on the other hand, the Party Secretary advised all partners to respect the policy statement made by the Chief Minister. Even after making the joint statement, the RSP continued to express dissent publicly on the Industrial Policy. Moreover, they added to the criticism saying that the UF government had failed to give the people sufficient relief even after 18 years of rule and that there was rampant corruption in the system.[33] Some RSP members went to the extent of demanding a party plenum to decide whether the party should remain in the UF government longer. The CPI also had its resentment about the big brotherly attitude of the CPI(M) as regards the decision-making process. Nevertheless Basu pushed through all opposition by standing firm on his ground and assigning the blame for such a stand to the Central Government.

On non-ideological issues too there were tensions between partners of the Left Front in recent times. The CPI decided in August 1995 to start a movement in support of Uniform Civil Code, and the unilateral decision was about to bring a jerk to the solidarity of the Front.[34] The Forward Bloc, generally more submissive than the RSP, accused the ruling front of developing "bourgeois vices".[35] This was a reflection of their differences with the CPI(M) over the question of sharing power in the Municipal Corporation. The CPI(M), as usual, decided to steamroll dissent and, in a meeting of the Left Front Committee served the ultimatum to its partners to either fall in line or perish.[36]

Internal dissensions made the LF partners comparatively weaker and sometimes the CPI(M) leadership had to intervene in resolving their conflicts. By the end of 1995, the FB and the CPI presented dismal pictures of houses divided against themselves.[37] Two FB Ministers — Kalimuddin Shams and Saral Deb — were facing charges of corruption and nepotism. The group led by Kamal Guha formed its own political outfit – the Forward Bloc (Socialist) — which threatened to cut into the party's vote bank. In the CPI a powerful member of Parliament, Guru Das Gupta, was at loggerheads with the State Secretary. Narayan Chaubey, a veteran expelled from the CPI, floated his own party and this was supposed to affect Inderjit Gupta's chances at Midnapore.

On the eve of elections to the Lok Sabha and the Legislative Assembly scheduled to take place in March 1996, the Left Front alliance gave a picture of infighting. There were demands for more seats on the part of the constituent parties like the CPI, Samajwadi Party, Democratic Socialist Party and the Communist Revolutionary League of India.[38] But these were two minor problems for the CPI(M) which controlled enough support in the House on its own. The rift within the FB was bridged for the time when Jyoti Basu asked the FB leader to accommodate the FB(Socialist) as a part of the election strategy. Basu took the initiative in bringing the two factions of the Forward Bloc together and in persuading them to an agreement in his presence.[39] This further weakened the FB(Socialist), for some prominent leaders including MPs and MLAs returned to the original party.

The Left Front coalition that contested the election together in March 1996 consisted of ten parties: CPI(M), CPI, FB, FB(S), RSP, SP, DSP, BBC, RCPI and CRLI. The LF won majority a fifth time now, but there was a decline of popularity as evidenced by the loss of 32 seats of the CPI(M), defeat of nine ministers, almost a complete rout in Calcutta and in the industrial belt, and a cut by half of Basu's majority. For the first time since 1977 there was a downswing in the party's popularity. The LF won 204 of 294 Assembly seats, with the CPI(M) getting 158 seats, and the Congress winning 82, almost doubling the 1991 tally.[40] Basu was sworn in as Chief Minister for the fifth time, with a 48-member Ministry having representation for all 13 districts of West Bengal. He continued as Chief Minister until November 2000, when he voluntarily retired with the permission of the party.

Co-ordination Committees

The formation of a common forum for co-ordinating the coalition partners in West Bengal can be traced back to the first experiment of coalition government in 1967. Within a week of the installation of the UF Ministry a Co-ordination Committee was set up with representatives of all constituent parties.[41] Each party was supposed to send two representatives to the meetings of the Committee, but in practice the number varied from one to five. Each party had only one vote. There was no fixed schedule of meetings and meetings were convened whenever required. The Committee used to discuss policy issues and public relations programmes; it was instrumental for settling inter-party and intra-government disputes; and it was supposed to guide and supervise the government. Issues relating to land reforms, labour, law and order and inter-party dispute dominated most of the deliberations of the Committee.

Such was the political importance assumed by the Committee that it came to be regarded as a "super Cabinet". In fact during the UF government of those days the Committee enjoyed a higher status than that of the Cabinet. Having had to co-ordinate parties which had irreconcilable differences — both ideological and non-ideological — the Committee came to be described as "ideological watch dog" of the UF partners. Nevertheless the UF Committee often served as a forum for mutual bickerings and slanderous attacks more than for effecting smooth co-operation. The cause for the friction lay in the fact that the UF Committee had to accommodate within it parties of diverse complexions and conflicting commitments.

The picture has been quite different since 1977. Under the CPI(M)-led governments, the role of the UF Committee, as the UF Co-ordination Committee came to be called, has been reduced considerably. Meetings of the Committee have been far less frequent than before.[42] And the LF Committee meetings often reflected the undercurrents of tension within the Front government. There were often allegations raised by the coalition partners against the CPI(M), the Front's overlord, about short-circuiting the LF Committee while taking decisions on major issues. This was evident from a letter sent by Asim Chatterji, CRLI leader, to Sailen Das Gupta, the LF Committee Chairman, pointing out that policy decisions were being taken without knowing the allies' mind.[43] Copies of the letter had been sent to Jyoti Basu, the Chief Minister, Biman Bose, the politbureau member and Anil Biswas, the Party Secretary. The CPI, FB and RSP were also reported to be thinking on Chatterjee's lines. The CPI was even planning to organise protests against a hike in power rates levied by Calcutta Electric Supply Corporation. There were similar instances earlier also when the partners had held protests against the government decisions. Nevertheless the Co-ordination Committee is considered to be important in the policy making and governing process.

Jyoti Basu and the Council of Ministers

Jyoti Basu was generally accepted as the top most leader of the CPI(M) since the split of the former Communist Party. And this was confirmed by his election as the leader of the CPI(M) Parliamentary party and Deputy Chief Minister of the first and second UF Ministries in the sixties. His continuous election as Chief Minister since 1977 has made him the undisputed leader of the party. He has thus combined control over the party and over the government which has given him tremendous power and political leverage in the State. In May 1996 Basu was sworn in as Chief Minister for the fifth time.

The Left Front government in West Bengal has been in effect a single-party government since 1977, CPI(M) having had enough majority to form a government of its own in successive elections. Still the party preferred to work in coalition with other like-minded parties in spite of occasional wranglings. The credit for taking all Leftist parties together for a smooth ride goes to none other than Jyoti Basu, the Chief Minister for more than two decades. He has been able to cement a unity among a class-oriented CPI(M), a party-based CPI, a self-conscious RSP, a self-proclaimed Revolutionary Communist Party (RCPI) and a faction-ridden Forward Bloc. It is Basu's personal success that has been keeping the Left Front coalition intact. There have been all throughout instances of high handedness among the CPI(M) cadres and big brotherly attitude among the party's top leaders, but the junior partners of the Left Front have had access to the Chief Minister and they have always felt at ease with him in dealing with inter party problems. He has been, sometimes, able to dictate decisions to the partners or go ahead irrespective of their stance. Through the six decades of his political career in the State and more than five decades in the State legislature, Basu has been able to create for himself a unique image of respectful acceptability to the common people, irrespective of their party loyalties. The fact that he had been chosen a consensus candidate for premiership by the first United Front at the Centre shows the degree of credibility he enjoys among the political parties in the country. His chances of becoming the first UF Prime Minister were spoiled by the unthinking rigid stance of the CPI(M) politbureau which decided not to join the Ministry.

Although a Marxist to the core, Basu's relationship with West Bengal-based industrialists has been one of co-operation and cordiality. Much of the foreign and Indian capitalist investment in the State has been facilitated by the involvement of Basu and the re-assurance of his remaining at the helm. Many of the CPI(M) and RSP cadres in the State have not yet reconciled themselves with the compulsions of industrialisation. Basu's continuance as Chief Minister is reassuring to the industrialists while no other leader can deal with them so amicably.

Basu has occasionally asserted himself so much so, he has been dubbed autocratic by his coalition partners. His commitment to modernisation of Calcutta has been too deep to be deterred by considerations for the poor and the oppressed. He had issued orders for allotting a 38-acre plot in Salt Lake to Globsyn-WEBEL, a joint sector company which was planning to build a Rs. 350-crore futuristic hi-tech software office-cum-residential complex to be called "Infinity — an Intelligent Village".[44] This was twice overruled by the Urban Development Minister Asim Das Gupta who wanted to use the land for rehabilitating the Bangladeshi refugee residents. On similar grounds Asim Das Gupta had refused to honour Basu's commitment to hand 59 cottahs of land in Ballyaganj Park Road to the External Affairs Ministry for building a modern branch secretariat. However, when it came to "Operation Sunshine", i.e. the eviction of about 60,000 hawkers from Calcutta streets, it could be carried out smoothly without any internal conflict in the Left Front. This had been included in the conditionalities attached to foreign assistance to transform Calcutta into a mega city.[45]

Basu has sometimes deliberately created confusion among his party ministers by violating the convention that the charge of Chief Minister's office should be handed over to the next senior man during his absence. This becomes a sensitive issue as it raises the question of the No. 2 position in the Cabinet. Budhadev Bhattacharya, generally considered the No. 2 man in the Cabinet, has sometimes been sidelined and charge given to other ministers.[46] This has caused heartburn among the ministers as well as in CPI(M) party circles. This led to the CPI(M) decision later to approve of Budhadev as No. 2 man in the Council of Ministers and enable him act as Chief Minister during Basu's trip to UK and South Africa in 1997.[47]

Basu has occasionally asserted himself in party matters as well as in Cabinet decision-making. He could force the State Committee of the party to revise a decision to remove the Transport Minister Subash Chakraborty from the North 24-Parganas District Committee of the party and get him reinstated.[48] In a similar situation some years ago Jatin Chakraborty and Budhadev Bhattacharya had to resign from Cabinet posts owing to differences with Basu, and Budhadev could come back only when Basu agreed to accommodate him.[49] There was also an instance of his personal choice being decisive in the selection of his ministers. Basu took personal initiative in inducting Sankar Sen into the Cabinet and making him the Minister for Power, despite the opposition of hardliners in the party. Sankar Sen was not a career politician and he could improve the power position in the State, although he later got involved in a public interest litigation against the State government.[50] Similarly it was considered a personal success of Basu when the latter managed to get the removal of Sailen Das

Gupta as the Party Secretary and appointed Anil Biswas to the same post.[51]

Despite factionalism and infighting in the party, Basu has been able to remain its most powerful supremo and charismatic leader. Infighting has been particularly serious in district committees adjoining Calcutta, the North and South 24-Parganas district committees.[52] In both these committees the tussle for power has led to intense bitterness between rival groups involving even ministers. Even a five-member high-power committee headed by Jyoti Basu could not resolve the differences.[53] Senior party leaders feel that 22 years of Left Front rule has made the CPI(M) abrasively authoritarian. They point out that there has been a slump in the work culture of government departments. The party identified government sectors like health, education, drinking water supply, road, water transport and public distribution system as low-performance areas.[54]

Nevertheless Jyoti Basu's leadership is undisputed in the party and is considered indispensable to the State. After two decades in office as Chief Minister, he expressed the desire to retire from active politics. But the party insisted on keeping him as Chief Minister. So the question of Basu's retirement was shelved for the time; Budhadev was appointed Deputy Chief Minister to reduce his office burden as well as to finally resolve the question of No. 2 position. Basu proved himself competent in holding the Left Front intact despite occasional confrontations with the partners. Industrialists in West Bengal felt confident about his credibility and reliability. Lord Swaraj Paul, a foreign industrialist, observed: "One of the key components of the Chief Minister's success has been his ability to combine vision with a flexible approach."[55] He added philosophically: "History tells us that leaders often fail not because of lack of ability or brain power; they often fail because of lack of maturity. Many could learn a lesson or two from Jyoti Basu's understanding and perspectives."

NOTES

1. Anjali Ghosh, *Peaceful Transition to Power* (Calcutta, 1981), p. 51.

2. P.R. Chaudhary, *Left Experiments in West Bengal* (New Delhi, 1985), pp. 60-65.
3. Anjali Ghosh, n. (1), p. 83.
4. *Ibid.*, p. 89.
5. P.R. Chaudhary, n. (2), p. 96.
6. Surabhi Banerjee, *Jyoti Basu : The Authorised Biography* (New Delhi 1997), p. 139.
7. *Ibid.*
8. Anjali Ghosh, n. (1), p. 109.
9. *Ibid.*, p. 115.
10. Surabhi Banerjee, n. (6), p. 145.
11. Anjali Ghosh, n. (1), p. 124.
12. *Ibid.*, p. 124.
13. Surabhi Banerjee, n. (6), p. 147.
14. Anjali Ghosh, n. (1), p. 127.
15. *Ibid.*, p. 136.
16. Surabhi Banerjee, n. (6), p. 149.
17. Anjali Ghosh, n. (1), p. 136.
18. *Ibid.*, p. 136.
19. *Ibid.*, p. 150.
20. Surabhi Banerjee, n. (6), p. 157.
21. *Ibid.*, p. 167.
22. Anjali Ghosh, n. (1), p. 167.
23. Surabhi Banerjee, n. (6), p. 174.
24. *Ibid.*
25. *Ibid.*, p. 176.
26. *Ibid.*, p. 183.
27. "From Breakdown to Order: West Bengal", in Partha Chatterjee (ed.) *State Politics in India* (OUP), 1997, p. 356.
28. *Ibid.*, p. 336.
29. P.R. Chaudhary, n. (2), p. 147.
30. *Hindustan Times* (New Delhi), 6 October, 1994.
31. Balraj Mehta, "An Ambivalent Approach", *Deccan Herald,* 28 October, 1994.
32. *Ibid.*
33. Ashis Chakrabarti, "It is One Party Rule in West Bengal", *Indian Express* (New Delhi), 9 August, 1995.
34. *Hindustan Times* (New Delhi), 11 August, 1995.
35. *The Statesman* (New Delhi), 15 August, 1995.
36. Sudhir K. Singh, "Tired and Brusque", *The Pioneer* (New Delhi), 17 August, 1995.
37. Tarun Ganguly, "Back to Front", *Telegraph,* 15 November, 1995.
38. *Hindustan Times* (New Delhi), 9 February, 1996.
39. *Telegraph,* 10 March, 1996.
40. *Patriot* (New Delhi), 29 May, 1996.
41. *Anjali Ghosh,* n. (1), p. 64.
42. Ashis Chakrabarti, n. (33).
43. *The Hindu,* 6 January, 1999, p. 15.

44. Manash Ghosh, "Minister over rules Basu's orders on land grant", *The Statesman* (New Delhi), 11 August, 1996.
45. *The Statesman* (New Delhi), 31 January, 1997.
46. *Telegraph* (Calcutta), 17 September, 1996; *The Pioneer* (New Delhi), 26 September, 1996.
47. *Telegraph,* 28 January, 1997.
48. *The Pioneer* (New Delhi), 20 August, 1998.
49. *National Herald* (New Delhi), 12 November, 1999.
50. *Telegraph,* 10 November, 1998.
51. *Telegraph*, 20 November, 1998.
52. *Hindustan Times* (New Delhi), 16 February, 1999.
53. *Ibid.*
54. *Telegraph,* 17 February, 1999.
55. *Times of India* (New Delhi), 8 July, 1999.

6

IMPACT OF COALITION POLITICS ON PARLIAMENTARY INSTITUTIONS — The Indian Experience

India, having adopted a parliamentary structure of government within a federal system, has constitutionally provided for parliamentary structures at both the Centre and in the States. The same principles and norms of parliamentary practice are applied at both levels substantially. Innovations experimented and successfully operated at the Centre or in anyone of the States may be accepted as models or precedents by the rest whenever found useful.

It is largely the Westminster model of parliamentary structures that the Indian Constitution has adopted for both the Central and State governments. But the Indian political culture being different from that of the UK, the structures have had to be functionally modified. India being a vast subcontinent with innumerable culturally and ethnically diverse groups, political behaviour within the country has proved to be different from region to region or State to State. Ethnic loyalties and cultural diversities have tended to produce political behaviours different from each other, but within the same constitutional and legal framework. Therefore although the legal framework is uniform throughout the country, political behaviour and practices tend to be different.

The constitutional system envisages a majoritarian form of parliamentary government in India at the Centre and the States, more or less like the British. However the political reality has brought about multiple parties resulting in governments of party coalitions or alliances. The Congress party emerging from the national movement and seeking to represent a national consensus on political programmes and ideology wished to provide governments for the Centre and all the States for all time to come. But the majoritarian single-party governments became an impossibility with the breakdown of the Congress and with the inability of the other parties to provide a single-party alternative being established. Although the Congress party has shown unwillingness to share power with other parties at the Central Government, it has permitted its State units to do so and thus participated in coalition governments early in the fifties. The Congress party of the erstwhile Travancore-Cochin State had been compelled to share power with the Tamil Nadu Congress and the Socialists in 1952 and in 1954. The political developments in Kerala since 1960 were results of coalition games centred on two major political parties — the Congress and the CPI(M). The communal equation had established the predominance of Nair and Christian communities in Travancore-Cochin State. The merger of Malabar and the formation of Kerala State shattered this equation and led to the considerable rise of Muslim and Ezhava power in the State. Thus the change in communal equation produced its impact on the politics of the State and this appears to be the underlying factor of power politics in the State.

West Bengal was under Congress rule until 1967 when the party's grip was crippled and the Communists started rising in popularity. For one decade since 1967, West Bengal underwent a traumatic experience of governmental instability and political violence, and finally got settled under the leadership of the CPI-(M). Thus while Kerala has been practising coalitional politics for more than 40 years, West Bengal has experimented it for about 30 years and achieved stability since 1977.

The year 1967 marked a watershed in Indian politics as about eight States had formed non-Congress coalition governments. The Congress' dominance in Indian politics clearly broke in several States and the party had to sit in the Opposition. Although the Congress could regain power in some of these States, its popularity throughout the country was further eroded. The Congress lost power at the Centre within a few years and although it could come back in full glory it was doomed to lose it again. It lost control of more States in succeeding years so much so there were non-Congress coalition governments in fourteen States in 1997. The number of States that opted for coalition governments was increasing from 1967, but all States were not steady in the path of coalitions in this period. States like Rajasthan and Madhya Pradesh went back to Congress rule, while new States embarked on coalition experiment. Some States like Orissa, Maharashtra, Punjab, Bihar and Goa went back and forth between single-party rule and coalition rule. The steady decline of the Congress and the absence of another strong party to take its place either at the Centre or in the States in general has brought the coalition system to stay as a prevailing mode in the end of the 1990s.

The coalitional experience within the framework of Westminster model parliamentary structures, based on the present study, may be summed up as follows :

(i) Coalition governments in a parliamentary system are not necessarily unstable. Stability depends on several factors.

(ii) Coalition politics compel deviations and innovations in the parliamentary model to suit the needs of the coalition system.

(iii) The areas wherein coalition politics have made noticeable impact are broadly the Executive, the Legislature and the Party system.

Early writers used to presume that coalition politics undoubtedly led to short-lived governments, and they preffered statistics to prove the same. Their treatises failed to analyse the multi-dimensional causes involved and tended to make the inferences biased. E. Sreedharan points out four sets of factors that affect the stability of coalition governments.[1] First, the regime-level attributes or the institutional structures within which coalitions are formed. These include the fragmented character of the parties, the effective number of parties, the degree of ideological polarization, the opposition's access to policy influence, the legal provision for elections in case of a government collapse and the provision for a constructive no-confidence vote as well as for a formal confidence vote after investiture. Second, the attributes of the coalition itself, such as the majority or minority status of the coalition, the number of parties in the coalition, its ideological cohesiveness, etc. Third, the nature of the ideological spectrum, that is, whether the coalition is ideologically single-polar, bi-polar or multi-polar. Fourth, the incidence of any political event that creates diverging reactions among members of the coalition. Gregory M. Luebert points to the kind of compromise reached between partners on the basis of their respective policy profiles as the key to stability.[2]

The above observations based on Western theories are presumed to be universalistic in character and application. But the Indian society and politics do not fit into the Western framework. In the Indian situation, the present study leads to certain inferences which may be listed as follows :

1. Coalitions cut across Left-Right, communal-secular national-regional divisions with the chief pursuit of office as the only reality.
2. Coalition between an anchor party and satellite parties tends to be stable.
3. Among such coalitions, if the anchor party commands a majority by itself as in West Bengal, it is likely to be stabler. A coalition of mutually dependent parties (that is, no party having a majority on its own) also is likely to be durable as in Kerala. Of the two categories mentioned, the former is likely to be stabler.
4. Minority coalitions, propped up by external support whether conditionally or unconditionally, are not likely to be stable.
5. The anchor party tends to make more than proportionate concessions to the smaller ones who gain more than proportionately to their strength.
6. Factions within the parties, particularly the anchor party, threaten the stability of the coalition.
7. Factional splits tend to be accommodated in the pursuit of office-seeking interest.
8. Surplus majority or large-size coalitions are stabler than minimal-winning coalitions.

9. Political cultures of Indian States vary, and some are more conducive to stable coalition politics than the others.

The impact made on the Executive, the Legislature and the Party System may be analysed separately with respect to each area and the consequences assessed.

The Executive

The three dimensions of the parliamentary executive that are influenced by coalition politics are: Cabinet formation, Cabinet management and the nature of the Cabinet. The institutional and legal, the political and personal dimensions of the Cabinet system get interlinked with the two basic processes of the parliamentary executive, viz. Cabinet formation and Cabinet management. The majoritarian Cabinet and the coalition Cabinet, being different as regards the above three dimensions, tend to produce different impacts on the two processes and their results. The Constitution envisages, as already pointed out, a majoritarian government of the British model and provides for a parliamentary government. Article 74 and Article 163 respectively state that there shall be a Council of Ministers with the Prime Minister/Chief Minister at the head to aid and advise the President of India/Governor of the State in the exercise of their functions. According to the parliamentary practice the leader of the majority party in the Parliament/State Legislature becomes the Prime Minister/Chief Minister and he in turn selects his colleagues in the Council of Ministers.

In coalition politics, the leader of the leading party is usually elected as the leader of the parliamentary party of the coalition, but he shall be acceptable to the allies as well. Sometimes the leader of a minority party may be chosen by the coalition to head the Cabinet. The general principle seems to be that the head of the Cabinet, whatever the degree of standing he has in his own party, shall be acceptable to all partners of the coalition whose will may turn out to be decisive in the matter of electing the Prime Minister/Chief Minister. It is generally observed that the general election to the Parliament or the State legislature is today the occasion for electing the Prime Minister/Chief Minister also, as the whole election process is centred round the leader of the party or alliance of parties. But in a coalitional set up the post-election situation can upset the earlier arrangements.

As regards the appointment of the Council of Ministers, Article 75(1) and Article 164(1) of the Constitution say that the Prime Minister/Chief Minister shall be appointed by the President/Governor and that the other Ministers shall be appointed by the President/Governor on the advice of the Prime Minister/Chief Minister. The traditional practice is that the Prime Minister/Chief Minister will choose the Ministers by paying due weightage to various factors to be considered. In coalition politics in India the Ministers are chosen by the respective parties themselves, and the Prime Minister/Chief Minister may not have a say in normal circumstances. This situation further weakens the position of the Prime Minister/Chief Minister in relation to his own party, particularly if it is ridden with factionalism. There are instances of Prime Ministers and Chief Ministers being dictated to by factions in their own party about appointing some members as Ministers or even about avoiding the appointment of somebody whom they do not like to be with them in the Cabinet. This is possible in a single-party government also, but in a multi-party government the Prime Minister/Chief Minister is comparatively weaker.

Coalition is a bargaining process between the partners, and the process is on-going from the start to the finish. The representation of the partners in the Ministry, the allocation of proportionate seats and the distribution of portfolios among them often occasion serious bargaining. It is admissible if the major parties get a bigger share as they can be supposed to have a bigger stake in election campaigns and a greater responsibility in administration. But it often happens in India that the smaller parties plead for a disproportionately larger pay off in terms of the number and importance of positions, and they often succeed in winning them. This is particularly so when the leading party is dependent on the minor parties for the maintenance of the coalition. The minor partners seem to presume that it becomes solely the responsibility of the leading party to preserve the coalition and they behave in irresponsible ways very often. So to say, the leading party becomes the loser in the bargaining game as it has to give up a part of its due share in order to satisfy the bullying partners. It must be surprising that in some coalitions, all MLAs of a partner party are made Ministers in order to prop up the Ministry.

As regards distribution of portfolios there is always fight for 'plum posts' like Finance, External Affairs, Railways and Defence at the Centre and for similar prestigious portfolios in State Governments. Such distribution can be arranged to the satisfaction of all parties only by a process of negotiation and compromise. Compromise can be arrived at through inter-party discussions or discussions in the co-ordination committees. Issues like distribution of portfolios can be settled most effectively by co-ordination committees. Any discontentment left in this regard may crop up again and create fresh crises now and then which may even lead to destruction of the coalition. Hence distribution of portfolios is a very delicate task for the Prime Minister/Chief Minister in a coalition demanding astute handling.

The demand for larger representation and better portfolios is likely to create funny situations as regards the size of the Cabinet. The number of Ministers may go on increasing as the 'accommodating spirit' waxes, and one may wonder if a poor country like India can afford to have so many Ministers to govern them. On the basis of the recommendation of the Karan Singh Committee (1992) it was generally accepted that ministerial positions should not exceed one-tenth of the strength of the lower house concerned. But this has been violated by Chief Ministers like Kalyan Singh of UP and Rabri Devi of Bihar who offered to make Ministers of all defectors in order to win their support to prop up the Ministry.[3] Members of the Lok Tantrik Congress party who formed the new party after crossing floor from the Congress(I) were all Ministers in Kalayan Singh's Ministry and later in R.P. Gupta's Ministry. Some of them had only very minor portfolios or had no portfolios at all.

Once the Council of Ministers is formed, there arises the problem of co-ordinating them and pulling them together. As they belong to different political parties, the Ministers may have different or even contradictory opinions, interests and visions.

The foremost characteristic of a coalition Ministry is the absence of political homogeneity. As such, the management of ministerial colleagues and monitoring of their activities call for extraordinary competence and patience on the part of the Prime Minister/Chief Minister.

The Cabinet system of UK has historically evolved the character of collective responsibility. The Indian Constitution has legalised this character in Article 75(3) and Article 164(2) which state that the Council of Ministers shall be collectively responsible to the Lower House. 'Collective responsibility' implies that all Ministers hold themselves responsible for all decisions of the Cabinet and that, once a decision is formally taken by the Cabinet, each Minister has the obligation to defend it publicly. Even if someone has a dissent with the collective decision, the dissenting view is expected to be suppressed or kept in reserve for the time. This aspect was emphasised by the Supreme Court when the latter expressed 'distress' and 'concern' over some Statements of Ram Jethmalani, the Central Law Minister in Vajpayee's second Ministry, which appeared contradictory to an affidavit filed in the court by the Government of India.[4] Jethmalani had to resign his post when he criticised the Chief Justice of India and the Attorney-General following the above observation of the Supreme Court. The Prime Minister had to admit in the Rajya Sabha that the Law Minister was not willing to submit himself to the discipline of collective responsibility and that on a number of occasions he had spoken out on matters that did not pertain to his ministerial responsibilities.[5]

There are umpteen number of instances wherein dissent has co-existed with collective responsibility in the various coalition governments. The CPI and the Forward Bloc in West Bengal could not agree with the new industrial policy of the CPI(M), but they decided to remain in government. In West Bengal the coalition partners had sometimes led agitations against the government of which they were a part. Further there were often intra-coalition dissensions in West Bengal and Kerala when one party was threatened by the growth of power on the part of another. On the eve of elections, they came to open clashes on the distribution of seats between them. In recent times the country has witnessed the PMK and MDMK ministers of the NDA government openly dissenting with the Central Cabinet's collective stand on Sri Lanka.[6] Hence the concept of collective responsibility in its classical form needs to be made flexible in the coalitional structure of government. Political homogeneity being the first victim of coalition governments, an agreement to accommodate dissent becomes inevitable.

In majoritarian governments there is no institution other than the Cabinet to formulate policies and co-ordinate Ministries or departments of government. The party machinery exercises control over the Prime Minister/Chief Minister and other Ministers directly. But in a coalition Ministry consisting of several parties, there is no single-party machinery which can control all of them. Ministers belong to several parties and their future political prospects rest with their own parties. In such circumstances it is quite rational to evolve a separate forum for bringing the coalition allies together to discuss policy matters. In other words, institutionalized bargaining structures become relevant in coalition politics. However, there have been instances of the Co-ordination Committee becoming too powerful as a super Cabinet and interfering in administrative matters. As it is an extra-constitutional body of informal origin it is necessary to watch and control its growth so as not to infringe upon the constitutional status of the Cabinet. At the same time it is equally necessary to see that it is not neglected, as often complained by allies, and it has to be kept on an even keel. It is important that all coalition partners cultivate an attitude of respect towards the Co-ordination Committees. It is therefore advisable to provide for a constitutional status to the Co-ordination Committees in case of coalition governments.

The idea of an all party national government was suggested time and again, since 1989, in the context of a single-party failing to get majority in the Lok Sabha.[7] One of the suggestions envisaged the election of the Prime Minister by the Lok Sabha by means of single transferable vote from among candidates (not necessarily members of Parliament) who would secure support of at least 100 Lok Sabha members. The Council of Ministers would consist of representatives of all parties in proportion to their strength in the House. A common minimum programme acceptable to all or most parties should be placed before both houses of Parliament and approved. A no-confidence motion passed against the government should be effective only after the election of an alternative Prime Minister. Other suggestions included that :

(i) the Prime Minister be elected by the Lok Sabha and shall resign only when an alternative leader is chosen;
(ii) the Prime Minister be elected by 2/3rd majority of the Lok Sabha;
(iii) the Prime Minister be elected by a majority of the Lok Sabha and Rajya Sabha;
(iv) the Prime Minister be elected by a majority of the Lok Sabha and Rajya Sabha and be removed only by 2/3rd majority in both houses; and
(v) the Prime Minister be elected by a simple majority of the Lok Sabha and a no-confidence motion passed by 2/3rd majority of the Lok Sabha.

The above suggestions are meant to be applied in a multi-party situation where no single-party is able to form a government. In such a situation the choice of Prime Minister or leader of the coalition shall be determined by a process of member participation and not by the party caucus. But any amendment of the existing system shall be done without violating the spirit of parliamentary process. The present coalition system, not being anti-parliamentary or non-parliamentary, the most that can be advised to be done by way of constitutional amendment is to see that the Prime Minister is not removed without ensuring the election of an alternative leader to be sworn in.[8]

Coalition is the dexterous execution of a tight-rope balancing, involving compromise between two or more distant or even contrary stand points. The deciding factor may be the payoffs emerging out of the bargaining process. Since each partner wants to take more for itself and give less to the other partners in the coalition, the centrally located parties are at an advantage in coalition bargaining.[9] It may theoretically be argued that larger parties possess better bargaining power because of their conspicuous presence and leadership status.[10] But this is not always proved in practice, and in the Indian situation smaller parties are found to be enjoying a disproportionately larger share in the arrangements. The leading party in the ruling coalition is often forced to part with its favourite choice to satisfy the smaller parties. And some of the latter like the AIADMK in the 1998 BJP-led government, the Trinamul Congress in the 1999 BJP-led government, or like the Muslim League and the Kerala Congress parties in Kerala which are prepared for a brinkmanship game extract larger chunks. Among the perks that the parties fight for are included not merely the ministerial portfolios, but membership of committees, membership of delegations and anything that shows off a higher status or superiority. In the present system of arrangements at the Centre, the BJP is at a disadvantage when compared to the other partners of the coalition. Out of the eleven committee Chairmen of the Lok Sabha the BJP has only one whereas the Congress(I), the leading party of the opposition, has two. And out of six Rajya Sabha Committees, the BJP has two Chairmen and the Congress (I) two. In parliamentary delegations, the minor partners get more than proportionate number of representatives. It may also be noted that in the seating arrangements of the Lok Sabha, the BJP does not have a proportionate number of seats in the front row of the chamber.

Since the objective of the partners is to maximize their position and power within the government, it is presumed that they behave in a rational manner. But the bargaining game is not always as rational as it is presumed to be and as such, the durability of the coalition could be in jeopardy. The bargaining process is made more complex by the involvement of more players like factions within the parties themselves. This is made worse when two factions of the same party hold opposite views about joining a coalition.

Sometimes there may be mini-coalitions within the larger coalition and they may function with the objective of wresting out special favours for them. Special common interests developed by a few partners thus forming a mini-coalition run against the general interests of the government and may ultimately end up in the ouster of the government. The 'federal front' formed under the leadership of Chandrababu Naidu within the United Front government, and the mini-front led by C. Achutha Menon in Kerala forming the government after the overthrow of E.M.S. Namboodiripad Ministry on 1 November, 1969 exemplify this tendency.

It is sometimes observed that two political parties representing the same social divisions or having the same ideological roots may find it more difficult to form an alliance or coalition than for two parties representing different social bases.[11] But it is equally well said that likeminded parties, that is, parties having the same background or philosophy are likely to coalesce more easily than parties with differing background or philosophy. Both arguments hold good, although apparently contradictory, but the success of coalition making depends on the nature of bargaining conditions. And once the coalition has been forged, the social cleavages and ideological nearness do not matter.

The Legislature

Structurally, coalition politics has not brought about any change in the Parliament or State legislatures. The parliamentary functionaries remain the same, and the rules of procedure and conduct of business also do not change. There are as many parliamentary parties and whips as there are political parties represented; and there will be a joint parliamentary party for the whole alliance whether ruling or in opposition.

Committees will be constituted and monitored under the same norms as they exist in parliamentary practices. Bills can be passed if the required majority is forthcoming as per rules. Constitutional amendments may be severely hampered or pushed back when it becomes difficult to muster two-third majority without the backing of the opposition. When the coalition gains a two-third majority on its own, it has still the burden of carrying all the coalition partners with it.

In a parliamentary system of government, it was the Parliament that originated as the centre of power, the Cabinet being dependent on and responsible to the Parliament. As time lapsed, the Cabinet appropriated political power and importance, and the governmental system came to be described "Cabinet dictatorship". The growth of the importance of the Prime Minister, centralisation of power in his hands and the consequent subjugation of the party and the ministers to the Prime Minister justified the sobriquet of "Prime Ministerial" government for the same parliamentary system. However, the changes were indicative of the trends in the paradigm shift of legislature-executive relationship in the parliamentary system. The emergence of coalition politics and the consequent weakening of the Prime Ministerial position tended to effect a change in the role of the Parliament in relation to the executive.

The coalition partners, being participants in the government, are supposed to provide it solidity and be collectively responsible for its performance. But being different in origin and character, they often make for dissent and mutual criticism. Thus a coalition government has also a built-in mechanism for mutual checks and balances. However, the actual performance of coalitions deviate from the idealistic vision of smooth collaboration and friendly dissent. They sometimes break into open fights on the floor of the house and outside. Any observer of the conduct of business in the Lok Sabha will be struck by the behavioural contrast of the members during the Congress regime and the post-Congress coalition period. The incidence of unruly behaviour in both houses of Parliament has been more frequent during the latter, and the Speaker has been compelled to convene meetings of parliamentary party leaders more often than before to settle quarrels. This points to the absence of a centralised parliamentary party organisation in a coalition system when contrasted to a single-party majority.

From a sociological point of view, this phenomenon is reflective of a general decline in the elitistic character of the people's representatives. Legislators speak in the language of the masses and behave in a style understandable to them. They come from the grassroots and represent the popular culture unlike the legislators of the fifties and sixties who represented a higher level culture. Moreover, with innumerable parties represented in the Parliament and State legislatures, the MPs/MLAs feel themselves closer to their respective party chiefs and immediately responsible to them unlike in the days of the

Congress-dominance system. The party chiefs behave like feudal lords and demand total loyalty from their legislators. The latter are dependent on their leaders for their career and future political existence. Today the legislators' freedom of speech in the legislature is restrained by the party leadership even though no legal provision provides for it.[12]

The Opposition may also be a coalition as in Kerala or it may consist of disunited single parties or groups of parties as in West Bengal or at the Centre. In either case one major function of the Opposition appears to be to entice the ruling coalition partners into their fold, not only to pull down the government but to strengthen their ranks. So the Opposition is never satisfied with attacking the policies of the government as in an orderly parliamentary system, but it is always alert on using other means for overthrowing the ruling coalition. Both sides being coalitions, it may be presumed that they are easily susceptible to efforts to make wedges in their blocs. Relatively, the Opposition of the coalition system at the Centre has become more powerful than that of the earlier Congress system.

The Party System

Coalition politics centres round political parties as it involves games played by the latter to gain the maximum pay off. It becomes relevant when no single-party is able to reach power by itself. In such circumstances one party joins another one or more parties to fight the elections and/or to form a government. The word 'coalition' originates from the Latin word 'coalitio' which means 'growing together'. Coalition is basically an alliance of parties that decide to work together in the election process or after the elections and share power in running the government.

Coalitions or party alliances may be pre-election or post-election phenomena. Some parties may cluster together, pool their resources and work jointly to maximise their gain by defeating the rivals in the election process. If there is a single alliance fighting against individual rival parties, the possibility of the alliance winning more seats than the rivals is stronger. If two equally strong alliances are pitted against each other, the effect will be that of a strong two-party system, either of them getting a majority to form the government. If more than two alliances contest, the result will be either in favour of one of them or none at all, with no alliance being able to win a majority. In the last situation, a government is possible only by means of a further coalition of two or more alliances.

1. Single alliance *vs.* Disunited parties
2. First alliance *vs.* Second alliance
3. First alliance *vs.* Second alliance *vs.* Third alliance

In West Bengal the Left Front alliance has come to be established as dominant in the State Legislative Assembly elections since 1977. In all successive elections after 1977 the Left Front remained united as a broad-based coalition whereas the Congress(I) — the leading party in the opposition — had failed to forge an effective alliance. In Kerala, the almost total victory of the *Saptamunnani* led by CPI(M) in 1967 against a disunited opposition convinced all parties of the need of an alliance for winning an election. Since 1967 no election was fought in Kerala without at least two alliances. In the 1970 election to the Legislative Assembly there was a Third Front in addition. However, the phenomenon of bipolarisation has appeared in Kerala politics with the emergence of two alliances — the LDF and the UDF — which may reasonably be described as a "two-party system within a multi-party system". The two-coalition model presented by Kerala State ensuring the possibility of alternative governments appears, theoretically, preferable to the single coalition dominance of West Bengal.

In the general elections to the Lok Sabha in 1996 there was a multi-cornered contest, with no strongly built alliance on the national scene. The BJP had a semblance of an alliance with three minor parties; the Congress(I) almost fought it alone; and the National Front and the Left Front could not agree on a Third Front. The result was a fragmented Parliament with none being able to form a government of its own. The BJP being the largest party was given a chance but they could not muster enough support. The post-election efforts brought the NF and the LF together to form a United Front and stake claim to form a government with the outside support of the Congress(I). Thus the United Front led by Deve Gowda consisting of thirteen parties was a post-election coalition formed temporarily to keep the BJP out of power. The UF-Congress(I) collaboration could not last beyond one year and a half as there was no common interest between them, and they soon fell as under.

In the next Lok Sabha elections of 1998, the BJP alliance had expanded its base to include sixteen parties, most of them region-based. The UF consisting of thirteen parties while in power lost its cohesion and had no accepted leader. The Congress(I) was still hesitant about a national level alliance, but was a bit rejuvenated owing to the "Sonia factor". Comparatively, the BJP-led alliance was more strongly united and more regionally based than the other two, and the election results proved the same. The BJP was determined to continue the alliance, with necessary modifications, in spite of internal contradictions. The National Democratic Alliance was forged sufficiently early to prepare for the electoral confrontation in 1999. It is apparent that in the present vortex of political relations in India coalitions are unavoidable.

What is the role of policy in coalition politics? According to M. Laver, political parties make use of policy packages as store fronts to attract voters and the leaders may forget them once the election is won.[13] Riker and Laver do not consider policy even as an instrument in electoral politics and coalition formation.[14] Anthony Downs said that parties formulate policies in order to win elections rather than win elections to formulate policies.[15] However, that a well-drawn-out policy and an air of commitment to implement the same will help maintain long-term credibility of the party or coalition of parties is nowhere doubted.

Coalition involves a commitment on the part of the political parties concerned to implement a pragmatic common programme, however, much ideologically at poles they are. Partners should agree on a common minimum programme of action, the implementation of which becomes the objective of sharing power. This involves 'ideological compromises' on the part of radical and fundamenalist parties. Sometimes rightist and leftist parties come together to stall a common enemy. Or it may be a coalition of secularists and communalists or even of Marxists and anti-Marxists. In either case there must evolve a common programme for positive action. The negative objective of pulling down a government or preventing a party from coming to power cannot succeed in bringing about a coalition. When 'like minded parties' or parties with similar ideological goals make a coalition, the making of a common programme may not have serious setbacks. Serious problems occur when ideologically polarised parties are forced to work together. The common minimum programme becomes a common manifesto for all parties that join the coalition. It cannot be the sum total of all the manifestos of the individual parties which may include contradictory ideas and promises. The common minimum programme (CMP) manifests compromise, and the minimum that the partners agree upon.

With a view to accommodating the ideologically distant parties, many ideological or 'fundamentalist' sacrifices will have to be made by the leading parties. Long standing coalitions will recognise the importance of CMPs and prepare them sufficiently early to face the elections. Hurriedly patched up coalitions often make hotch-potch agreements, without deep understanding between them, to forge a common programme like the National Agenda of the UF of 1996 or of the BJP-led coalition of 1998. According to Ajay K. Mehra, the Deve Gowda government had developed a CMP which was based not only on the manifestos of the coalition partners, but also incorporated the political agenda of those parties which had not participated in the government.[16] The CMP was only a broad statement of approaches to deal with India's problems. The BJP-led coalition of 1998 elections thought of framing a CMP after the elections and set-up a drafting committee with George Fernandes as convener for the purpose.[17] The document, called the National Agenda and prepared by Govindacharya, a General Secretary of the BJP, under direct inputs from Vajpayee, Advani and Fernandes, sought to avoid the politics of confrontation and usher in an era of national reconciliation and consensus.[18] The BJP sensed the growing returns from appearing moderate and accommodating. The BJP had to change its stance on some contentious issues like reconstruction of the Ram Temple at Ayodhya, introduction of a Uniform Civil Code and the deletion of Article 370 which gave special status to the Jammu and Kashmir State. These items were dropped from the CMP of the coalition government. This was a serious let-down for the BJP which had tried to build up the party organisation on this plank. Moreover the AIADMK which was an ally in the election refused to give a letter of support to the BJP to form the government until some of its unreasonable demands were incorporated into the agenda.[19] The AIADMK leader Jayalalitha had put forth five conditions : (i) dismissal of DMK government in Tamil Nadu; (ii) Central Finance Ministry to go to Subramanian Swamy; (iii) implementation of Cauvery Tribunal Award immediately; (iv) making Tamil an official language; and (v) allowing States to have their own reservation policy. She also wanted to be put on the agenda a demand for raising the height of the Periyar dam in Kerala to 150 feet. In such circumstances the process of preparing the CMP could be an impossible task. However, preparation of the CMP is also a strategy of making the partners acceptable to each other.

In the 1998 elections to the Lok Sabha the UF brought out a CMP and a joint policy statement on behalf of its partners, but the Left parties issued a separate manifesto highlighting their differences with the UF.[20] In Kerala State, in the 1967 Legislative Assembly elections, the seven-party Left Democratic Front had adopted a minimum programme for the first time and continued the practice in all successive elections.[21] The UDF also followed this practice and launched minimum programmes collectively. However, in the Assembly elections held in 1996 some of the coalition partners launched their individual programmes in addition to the common minimum programmes. This creates the interesting situation of the coalition projecting the minimum programme collectively and the maximum programme individually. This also reflects a lack of total faith in the coalition system as such.

In a single-member constituency multiple party system, small parties are not able to attain power by themselves and therefore they try to latch on to a bigger party for the purpose. In a single-member constituency system particularly, small parties fail to grow beyond their pockets of influence and their appeal is limited to their vote banks. So, in order to expand their sphere of influence or power they have to ally with other parties. At the same time each party is constrained by the other parties from growing into the areas of the latter. Thus coalition gives an opportunity for growth as well as it puts limits to growth. One party may try to break the limits by encouraging splits in other parties and weakening them. Internal splits destroy the parties themselves in the long run, but the split groups are accommodated for the time without destroying the coalition. The internal split of a coalition party, even when promoted by other coalition partners, may be treated apparently as an internal matter of the party concerned. The tendency to accommodate split groups help the smaller parties thrive in a coalition at the cost of the parent party, and they get disproportionate political leverage.

Personality-based factions and parties are a common phenomenon on the Indian political scene. This provides personality clash as a most common cause for party splits and in such cases any alliance between two newly emerging personality-centred parties becomes almost an impossibility, despite policy closeness or similarity of social base. Bitter hostility between the rival leaders and their followers may foreclose a meeting point, as in the cases of Karunanidhi *vs.* Jayalalitha, Laloo Prasad Yadav *vs.* Ram Vilas Paswan and Ramakrishna Hegde *vs.* Deve Gowda. But a common enemy or the lure of office may bring them together into the same coalition or another coalition after a lapse of time. Kerala State has witnessed a number of party splits resulting from personal ego conflicts as also their existence within the same coalition in view of remaining in office. The Kerala Congress is split into four parties, and three of them remain in the UDF as partners and one in the LDF. Ram Vilas Paswan has made his exit from the Janata Dal(U) — a partner of the NDA Ministry — and yet he collaborates with the parent party led by Sharad Yadav and remains in the NDA Ministry today.

Party coalitions in India always try to expand their base by attracting more parties than required for keeping themselves in power. That is, in other words, large-sized coalitions are a matter of attraction in the Indian situation. Following the tradition of the Indian National Congress in accommodating a large number of groups and interests, the party coalitions tend to make themselves '*Maha*-coalitions' for winning the largest number of seats for themselves and reduce the opposition to nil. So the ruling coalitions seem to be on constant search to pick and swallow from the opposition. At the Centre, a government can function effectively only if it is assured of two-third majority to make constitutional amendments possible. At the State level even a minimum majority can support the government in power and make it effective. Although minimum winning coalitions are applicable to State Governments, and not to the Central Government, the general tendency is to accommodate large-sized coalitions in the States also. This is a characteristic reflective of the political culture of the country.

Another phenomenon in Indian politics is the non-participating external support that some parties prefer to offer in order to prop up a party or coalition of parties in power without making a commitment to share the responsibilities of government. Parties think ahead about the consequences of their participation as regards the forthcoming elections to Parliament or regional elections to the State Assembly as well as about other reactions in State politics. And if they find the pay offs from immediate power lesser than the latent pay offs in store for them, they naturally prefer to stay off from immediate power. This has been the policy of TDP and Trinamul Congress towards the NDA government. However TDP was prepared to have a minimal participation by accepting the Speakership of Lok Sabha. This policy may result also from other covert considerations of the party leader such as stifling the growth of rival members in the party by blocking their entry into power positions. This further makes them feel free to declare their independence of the regime at slight provocations.

The political culture-coalitional politics linkage in the Indian situation is clear from the observations made in the above pages. What may be called the Indian political culture is a composite of heterogeneous, State-based political cultures further diversified by ethno-centric factors and evolutionary phases. The coalitional set-up is a political power relationship evolved from an all-inclusive, umberalla organisation of the Congress party and shaped by historical imperatives like the declining one-party dominance and Marxian change of attitude towards parliamentary palliative. But the common cultural elements may contribute to the emergence of stable political arrangements in most States of the country, if not in all.

Finally, the dependence of coalition politics on the electoral system needs to be examined. Maurice Duverger evolved a three-point thesis, from his analysis of European electoral politics, regarding proportional representation and the party system. The thesis included : (i) that proportional representation tends to lead to the formation of many independent parties; (ii) that the two-ballot majority system tends to lead to the formation of many parties that are allied with each other; and (iii) that the plurality rule tends to produce a two-party system.[22] Duverger's law has been examined at length, stimulating a whole body of research into the political consequences of electoral systems. But the impact of the plurality rule in the Indian situation has not been uni-dimensional or even bi-dimensional, being complicated by several factors such as ethnic divisions, economic cleavages and size of constituencies. The Italian experience of Proportional Representation compelled the revision of the electoral law in 1993, introducing plurality rule in three-quarters of the seats for Senate and Chamber of Deputies while retaining proportionality for the other part.[23] The first elections held in 1994 after the adoption of the new law witnessed a trend towards three alliances — Left, Right and Centre. But in contrast to Britain and the US, the Left and the Right were not unitarian political parties but loose alliances of very diverse parties. The experience of the Kerala State has been towards the creation and continuance of two alliances functioning more or less like a two-party formation. The plurality system's seat-vote disproportionality reinforces the stability of coalitions based on compromises. Disunity would mean to them vote disaggrgation and disproportionate loss of votes. Hence it follows that Duverger's thesis that the plurality rule system would tend to produce two-party system may be partly established in the situation wherein the opportunistic phase is crossed over.

NOTES

1. "Principles, Power and Coalition Politics in India : Lessons from Theory, Comparison and Recent History", in D.D. Khanna (ed), *Principles, Power and Politics,* Macmillan (New Delhi, 1999), pp. 275-77.

2. *Ibid.*
3. *The Hindu* (Thiruvananthapuram), 22 November, 1999.
4. *The Hindu* (Thiruvananthapuram), 22 July, 2000.
5. Harish Khare, "The Governance of Coalition Government", *The Hindu,* 30 July, 2000.
6. *Ibid.*
7. D. Sunder Ram (ed), *Coalition Politics in India,* NPH (Jaipur, 2000), pp. 253-54.
8. For a detailed analysis, see N. Jose Chander, "Coalition Politics and Constitutional Reform" in B.L. Fadia (ed) *Reviewing the Constitution,* Himanshu (New Delhi, 2001), pp.90-91.
9. Akhtar Majeed, "Coalitions as Power Sharing Arrangements", in Akhtar Majeed (ed), *Coalition Politics and Power Sharing*, Manak (New Delhi, 2000), p.7.
10. *Ibid.*
11. *Ibid.*
12. For a detailed study of party leader-legislator relationship, see Raju Abraham, *Role of Political Parties in State Legislatures* (New Delhi, 1999).
13. Cited in Akhtar Majeed, n. (9), p.16.
14. *Ibid.*
15. Anthony Downs, *An Economic Theory of Democracy*, Harper Row (New York, 1957), p. 28.
16. "The Cabinet System in a Coalition Situation", in Subhash C. Kashyap (ed), *Coalition Government and Politics in India* (New Delhi, 1997), p. 98.
17. *The Pioneer* (New Delhi), 15 March, 1998.
18. Swapan Das Gupta and Sabanaumi Bhaumik, "Crown of Thorns", *India Today,* 16 March, 1998, p. 16.
19. *Hindustan Times* (New Delhi), 13 March, 1998.
20. *The Hindu,* 2 February, 1998.
21. A. Balakrishnan Nair, *The Government and Politics of Kerala* (Thiruvananthapuram, 1994), pp. 168-69.
22. Maurice Duverger, *Political Parties* (London, 1986), p. 70.
23. Jug Steiner, *European Democracies*, 3rd edition, Longman (New York, 1995), pp. 87-88.

BIBLIOGRAPHY

Books

Abraham, Raju, *Role of Political Parties in State Legislatures*, New Delhi, 1999.

Banerjee Surabhi, *Jyoti Basu : The Authorised Biography*, New Delhi, 1997.

Bogdanor, Vernon (ed), *Coalition Governments in Western Europe*, London, 1983.

Chatterjee Partha (ed), *State Politics in India*, OUP, New Delhi, 1997.

Chaudhary P.R., *Left Experiments in West Bengal*, New Delhi, 1985.

Colomer, Joseph M. (ed), *Political Institutions in Europe*, Routledge, New York, 1996.

Dodd, Lawrence C., *Coalitions in Parliamentary Government*, Princeton, New Jersey, 1976.

Downs, Anthony, *An Economic Theory of Democracy*, Harper Row, New York, 1957.

Duverger, Maurice, *Political Parties*, London, 1986.

Fadia, B.L. (ed), *Reviewing the Constitution*, Himanshu, New Delhi, 2001.

Gandhi, Arun, *Morarji Papers*, New Delhi, 1983.

Gosh, Anjali, *Peaceful Transition to Power*, Calcutta, 1981.

John, John P., *Coalition Governments in Kerala*, Thiruvananthapuram, 1983.

Kashyap, Subhash C. (ed), *Coalition Government and Politics in India*, New Delhi, 1997.

Khanna, D.D. (ed), *Principles, Power and Politics*, Macmillan, New Delhi, 1999.

Khanna, S.K., *Coalition Politics in India*, Commonwealth Publishers, New Delhi, 1999.

Lane and Ersson, *European Politics an Introduction*, Sage, New Delhi, 1996.

Laver, Michael and Schofield, Norman, *Multi-party Government – – The Politics of Coalition in Europe*, OUP, New York, 1990.

Majeed, Akhtar (ed), *Coalition Politics and Power Sharing*, Manak, New Delhi, 2000.

Nair, Balakrishnan, A., *Government and Politics of Kerala*, Thiruvananthapuram, 1994.

Nossiter, T.J., *Communism in Kerala: A Study in Political Adaptation*, New Delhi, 1982.

Padhi, A.A. (ed), *Indian State Politics : A Case Study of Orissa*, B.R. Publishing Corporation, Delhi, 1985.

Pandey, Jawaharlal, *State Politics in India*, Uppal, New Delhi, 1982.

Prasannan, R. (ed), *Twentyfive Years of Kerala Legislature*, Thiruvananthapuram, 1983.

Ram, Sunder D. (ed), *Indian Parliamentary Opposition*, Kanishka, New Delhi, 1996.

_______ (ed), *Coalition Politics in India*, NPH, Jaipur, 2000.

Richardson, Bradley, *Japanese Democracy*, Yale University Press, New Haven, 1997.

Roy, Meenu, *Elections 1998*, NPH, Jaipur, 1999.

Singh Delip, *Dynamics of Punjab Politics*, Macmillan, New Delhi, 1981.

Steiner, Jug, *European Democracies*, Longman, New York, 1995.

Journals

Frontline
Outlook
India Today
Diary of Political Events
Politics India
The Link

Newspapers

The Hindu
Indian Express
Hindustan Times
Free Press Journal
Statesman
The Telegraph
The Pioneer
M.P. Chronicle
Times of India
Patriot
National Herald
Malayala Manorama (Malayalam)
The Desabhimani (Malayalam)
Kerala Kaumudi (Malayalam)
The Deepika (Malayalam)
The Mathrubhumi (Malayalam)

INDEX